THE
COMPLETE
MEATBALL
COOKBOOK

THE
COMPLETE
MEATBALL
COOKBOOK

Over 250 Mouthwatering Recipes from
Classic Italian Meatballs to Asian-Spiced Variations

Ellen Brown

CIDER MILL
PRESS

BOOK
PUBLISHERS

Kennebunkport, Maine

13-Digit ISBN: 978-1604334722
10-Digit ISBN: 160433472X

This book may be ordered by mail from the publisher. Please include $3.95 for postage and handling.
Please support your local bookseller first!

Books published by Cider Mill Press Book Publishers are available at special discounts for bulk purchases in the United States by corporations, institutions, and other organizations. For more information, please contact the publisher.

Cider Mill Press Book Publishers
"Where good books are ready for press"
12 Spring Street
PO Box 454
Kennebunkport, Maine 04046

Visit us on the web!
www.cidermillpress.com

Design by Alicia Freile, Tango Media
Typeset by Candice Fitzgibbons, Tango Media
Typography: Archer, Chaparral Pro, Helvetica Neue and Voluta
All images used under license from Shutterstock.com.
Printed in China

1 2 3 4 5 6 7 8 9 0
First Edition

Contents

Introduction

Who doesn't like meatballs? Meatballs are fun food, casual food, and flavorful food all rolled into one easy-to-eat morsel. And meatballs are so easy to make.

There isn't a cuisine that doesn't have a meatball of its own—even if it isn't made from meat. Call them *köttbullar* in Sweden, *keftedes* in Greece, or crab cakes in Maryland. The world loves meatballs. And this book lets you sample them all.

Meatballs are often thought of as "family fare" or "peasant food"—and with good reason. Add some vegetables, breadcrumbs, rice, or any other number of ingredients, and meatballs are a way to stretch a limited amount of expensive meat to feed more people. Now that's a concept that appeals to us today with skyrocketing food prices. Meatballs, however, can have much loftier culinary connotations. Take the French *quenelle*; it's nothing more than a poached meatball made with fish.

This book also contains many variations on the meatball theme. My theory is that after you make a recipe once and like the results, you'll want to make it again. You can make it exactly the same way, or you can change it up. For example, who doesn't love traditional Italian-American meatballs on top of spaghetti? But why not make lasagna with leftover meatballs?

Unlike most foods, meatballs also have dual personalities. They can be plain. They can be fancy. The same meatballs your family enjoys for dinner one night can be made as miniatures and served to guests as part of the hors d'oeuvres at your next cocktail party. Meatball dishes work well at buffets because they're "fork-only food." Even if larger than bite-sized, they can be divided into smaller pieces without using a knife, so guests can eat them easily while standing up.

So read on and start making—and enjoying—meatballs.

Chapter 1

Building the Best Meatballs

$\mathcal{M}$eatballs are good news for cooks. Why? It's almost impossible to mess them up. They're not like a soufflé that can turn into a flat pancake instead of reaching great heights. You don't need to be a professional chef with a battery of culinary skills. Meatballs are one of the easiest foods to make successfully, and in this chapter you'll learn the many ways there are to make them. You'll also learn ways to transform meatballs into other forms of foods such as a hearty meatball Shepherd's Pie or Meatball Lasagna, as well as general pointers on food handling that will make your kitchen a safer environment for all cooking.

My definition of *meatball* is a broad one: anything made from a mixture that is ground and ends up round is a meatball. Many of the recipes don't even use meat! There are meatballs made with poultry, fish, and vegetables— even sweet desserts.

Anatomy of a Meatball

Each ingredient in the ground mixture has a purpose, and together they produce a flavorful meatball with an appealing soft texture. While many meatballs are made the size of marbles or the size of golf balls, no one wants them to taste like either of those things. The ideal texture for a meatball is a soft interior; the exterior can be hard or soft depending on how they are cooked. Some of these ingredients play more than one role. For example, using rye bread for moisture adds flavor from the caraway seeds. Adding ketchup for flavor will also enhance the moisture in the mix.

Here are the various categories of ingredients that comprise a meatball, with some variations given:

* **The Starring Player:** The primary ingredient of a meatball is usually meat. But that can mean beef, veal, lamb, pork, poultry, or some combination of these. They can also be made with fish and shellfish. Grains, legumes, and vegetables can also take on the starring role but with a different touch than meat or seafood.

* **The Flavor Boosters:** This category includes herbs, spices, cheeses, vegetables, and prepared sauces and condiments. These ingredients vary in proportion by recipe; there are no hard and fast rules. If the meatball is intended to be eaten in a sauce, there will be fewer flavoring ingredients in the meatball itself, compared with those that are eaten off a toothpick as a stand-alone item. In addition to adding flavor, cheeses and condiments such as ketchup, mustard, or soy sauce also add moisture to meatballs. The vegetables in the meatball mixture can be either raw or cooked. Some combination of onion, celery, garlic, and carrots are most frequently used, but chopped mushrooms or mashed potatoes can be added as well.

* **The Seasonings:** Notice that specific amounts of salt and pepper aren't listed in the recipes because I believe this is a very personal decision. First make the meatball mix without salt and pepper before adding it because some of the secondary ingredients—such as seasoned breadcrumbs or condiments—may already include some salt and pepper. Season the mixture after all other ingredients have been added and blended.

* **The Texture Enhancers:** Most meatball recipes include at least one whole egg and sometimes an additional egg yolk or egg white. The egg serves as a binder for the other ingredients so the meatball holds its shape. The egg also offers a bit of fat and liquid to give the meatball a pleasing mouth feel when chewed. Some vegetables, such as cooked chopped spinach or shredded cooked carrots, also add texture to meatballs.

* **The Moisture Magnets:** In addition to liking meatballs with a soft interior, we also like meatballs that have a moist interior. That's where some sort of carbohydrate enters the picture. It can be anything from torn bread, fluffy Japanese panko, crushed crackers, or plain breadcrumbs to grains such as raw or cooked rice, oatmeal, or bulgur. The purpose of the carbohydrate is to absorb moisture as the meat cooks and gives off liquid.

Depending on what ingredient is used, the moisture magnet can also add to the flavor and texture to the meatball. Some recipes have a low moisture content, so the moisture magnet is soaked in a liquid before adding it to the mixture. In recipes with a high moisture content, the carbohydrate is added dry. The liquid in which it soaks can be as simple as water, to add only moisture to a recipe, or wine, stock, fruit juice, or tomato sauce to add flavor. Although each recipe in this book specifies a particular carbohydrate, feel free to change it or use whatever is on hand. Experiment. The only caveat is to determine if the moisture magnet was also contributing to the flavor of the meatball and adjust accordingly. For example, Italian pre-seasoned breadcrumbs are one of the great convenience foods on the market, but if all you have are plain breadcrumbs, add ½ teaspoon of Italian seasoning (or some combination of dried basil, oregano, and thyme) to the mixture per ½ cup of breadcrumbs used.

If you buy loaves of crusty bread on a regular basis, you can save money by making your own breadcrumbs. Once a loaf is a day old and the texture is no longer optimal, cut some of it into one-inch cubes and let it sit at room temperature for a day or so. Then place the rock-hard cubes in a food processor fitted with a steel blade and process until you have fine breadcrumbs. The bread can be a white baguette, a multi-grain, or flavored bread such as an olive or cheese loaf. Store the crumbs at room temperature in an air-tight container for up to one week.

The Daily Grind

The quality and type of ground meat makes an enormous difference when cooking beef meatballs because some cuts of beef are more flavorful than others. The best beef meatballs are made with ground chuck that is 80 percent lean and comes from a very well-marbled and flavorful cut. Should you want a leaner burger, look for ground sirloin. Avoid any packages generically labeled "ground beef."

The same distinctions are not made with other ground meats, such as pork or lamb. But in most supermarkets you do have the choice between ground turkey and all-white meat ground turkey. The all-white meat is a bit leaner but not as flavorful as the mixture that includes some dark meat. For meatballs made with a mixture of meats—usually beef, pork, and veal—many supermarkets carry a product called "meatloaf mix" containing all three meats in an equal proportion. I use this same proportion in many recipes in the chapter Double Your Pleasure: Meatballs with More Than One Meat.

Almost no one today actually grinds meat at home these days; my meat grinder lives in a box in the basement along with other culinary antiques such as my fish poacher and waffle maker. But chopping fish and seafood at home *is* necessary for some recipes, and there is no better friend than the food processor to accomplish this task.

For finfish, such as salmon, tuna, or cod, start by cutting the fish into 1-inch cubes, and arrange the cubes on a baking sheet lined with a sheet of plastic wrap. For shrimp, use the 21 to 25 shrimp per pound size. Remove and discard the shell, and devein the shrimp.

Place the baking sheet in the freezer for 20 to 30 minutes, or until the fish is partially frozen. Then transfer the cubes to the work bowl of the food processor and chop it either finely or coarsely, according to the directions in the specific recipe, using the on-and-off pulsing action.

In some recipes part of the chopped fish or shellfish is removed from the work bowl to add texture to the mixture, and the remainder is pureed with eggs to become the mousse-like base for the fish balls.

> There are actual recipes for meatballs from the time of the Romans. Marcus Gavius Apicius, better known as Apicius, was born in 25 CE, and his *De re coquinaria libri decem* (*Cuisine in Ten Books*) has an entire book devoted to "minces," or meat mixtures combined with other ingredients.

Putting It All Together

There is an order in which the various categories of ingredients are combined to create the best meatballs, although this may change to some extent from recipe to recipe. But remember this isn't rocket science. It's meatballs. And if you combine ingredients in an order other than the one specified in the recipe, your results will still be delicious.

Most recipes start by combining the ancillary ingredients and then adding the meat last. If the breadcrumbs or other carbohydrate are to soak in liquid, then that will be the first step. In a few recipes, any liquid remaining is discarded after the initial soaking time. If you don't have to drain away excess moisture, the recipe will begin by beating the egg with liquid and then adding the crumbs.

While the crumbs soak, the vegetables can be chopped and sautéed, if necessary, and the other ingredients can be assembled. If the vegetables are sautéed, they are then allowed to cool briefly so that they don't cook the egg when added to the mixing bowl. The last thing added is the meat itself, and then the mixture is formed.

The secret to achieving meatballs with lots of texture is to create a mixture with your fingertips—with clean hands or disposable plastic gloves. The ancillary ingredients are either chopped by hand or in a food processor using the on-and-off pulsing action so that the mixture is blended as briefly as possible and individual ingredients retain their characteristics. Using this method, the resulting meatballs are rustic and rarely form a perfect sphere because they are patted into shape rather than rolled between your palms.

For smooth and satiny texture, the mixture is beaten either in a food processor or in a standing mixer using a paddle attachment; hand mixers do not have enough power to beat a meat mixture into a smooth paste. I used both methods, depending on the recipe. But if you like smooth meatballs regardless of ingredients or sauce, use the food processor.

Once the mixture is together, it's time to taste for seasoning and add more salt and pepper, if necessary. Because almost all mixtures contain raw eggs, do not sample the mixture from the bowl. While it looks prettier if you fry up a small amount in a small skillet, I hate to dirty a pan for that task. I cook a few teaspoons, uncovered, in a microwave oven for 20 to 25 seconds. It will be pale and not very visually appealing, but it will be cooked through, and safe to sample.

If time permits, the flavor of meatballs is vastly improved if the mixture is refrigerated for at least one hour. In fact, it can be refrigerated for up to twelve hours, but after that should be cooked because it contains raw ingredients like meat and eggs that can be carriers of food-borne illnesses.

If you don't want to cook a meatball until it's well done, make the mixture without an egg. There are some recipes in this book made without eggs because their flavors and textures are improved if the meat is slightly rare. You can omit the egg and add more liquid to the mixture to replace the egg's role in providing moisture.

> A baseball player at bat loves being thrown a "meatball pitch," one that travels slowly through the upper part of the strike zone. It's an easy pitch to time and hit, often resulting in extra bases or even a home run.

From Mixture to Meatball

Whether your meatballs are the size of an egg yolk, the size of an egg, or the size of an orange, what's important is that the meatballs in each batch are all the same size so that they cook at the same rate. That might seem obvious, but it's actually harder to control than you think. With the repetition of forming meatballs they have a tendency to grow larger unless you're careful when portioning the meat.

It is faster to make meatballs—and forming them can take far more time than making the mixture from which they are formed— if you follow an assembly line process. First, measure your mixture out with an implement of specific size, and then turn the individual portions into balls.

For very small cocktail meatballs you can use the large side of a melon baller, and for slightly larger meatballs use a measuring tablespoon. Large meatballs can be formed in ¼-cup dry measuring cups, and there are specialized cookie dough scoops that come in a variety of sizes. These scoops are spring-loaded so they quickly discharge the mixture.

Once all the mixture has been portioned, it's time to form these blobs into meatballs. The easiest way is to *gently* roll the meat between the palms of your hands. Especially if you like meatballs with a lot of texture, the mixture should not be over-handled or it will negate all the good work you've done to give them texture. If you like meatballs with a smooth texture, roll the mixture into the perfect orb, but you will still have to do it gently because it is a soft mixture.

While serving cocktail meatballs on toothpicks—plain ones or those with frilly ruffles— is traditional, guests often don't know what to do with these sticks once the meatballs are consumed. Instead, use pretzel sticks or very thin carrot sticks as edible picks for the meatballs.

Cooking Strategies

In addition to being made from varied ingredients, meatballs are cooked in myriad ways. Some are fried; others are steamed. Some are grilled or broiled over very high heat while others are gently poached in barely simmering liquid.

Most meatballs are browned initially to create a crispy crust, but this can be done on a baking sheet in the oven or in a skillet on top of the stove. Some meatballs are coated with crumbs or a batter before they are cooked while others are cooked as they are.

The kind of mixture often dictates how the meatball should be eaten. Sometimes they are served without a sauce, so all the flavor is in the meatball itself. Other times they are simmered in a sauce (like the ubiquitous spaghetti and meatballs) or they are dunked into a dipping sauce.

One factor that remains constant is that meatballs are intended to be cooked through and not eaten rare, even those made from ground red meats that many people would eat rare as a steak or even as a burger. Since meatballs are made with eggs, eating uncooked or undercooked eggs can be dangerous from a health standpoint because eggs can be carriers of salmonella bacteria.

I am a firm believer that if one method requires constant attention while another method requires none of my attention, I'll always opt for the latter. I'd much rather be reading a book than turning meatballs in a skillet, and that's why the recipes in this book specify browning them in a hot oven. It happens all at once, and you're done with that step. If the meatballs are coated with crumbs, a light coating of vegetable oil spray will accomplish the same browning as the fat you would have in a skillet, and the crumbs absorb less fat.

But if you like to be more involved with your meatballs, brown them or cook them completely on top of the stove in a skillet. Use a 12-inch skillet or larger, and begin by adding enough vegetable oil to generously coat the bottom. Heat it over medium-high heat until a meatball sizzles loudly when placed in the pan. Then add the meatballs in a clockwise fashion starting at the top of the pan, being careful to leave at least 1½ to 2 inches between each.

Adjust the heat so that there is a merry sizzling sound and turn the meatballs gently after a few minutes so that all sides brown. The best implement to use is either a soup spoon or a pair of soup spoons, not a spatula that is too large to maneuver gracefully around the skillet. Do not turn the meatballs until a dark brown crust has formed on the side touching the pan. Because meatballs are round and the pan is flat, it is not easy to brown all sides evenly. Toward the end of the process, use one meatball as a prop for a neighboring meatball to keep it in the proper position.

Sizing Up the Situation

Each recipe in this book tells you what size to make your meatballs, but you can make your meatballs any size you wish. Here is some guidance for measuring the mixture:

* The large side of a melon baller produces a 1-inch meatball.
* A level measuring tablespoon produces a 1½-inch meatball.
* A heaping measuring tablespoon produces a 2-inch meatball.
* A ¼ cup dry measuring cup produces a 2½ to 3-inch meatball.

Perhaps you want to try a recipe that yields 2-inch balls but you want to serve them smaller and hors d'oeuvre-size at a cocktail party. Look for a similar recipe that makes 1-inch balls, which are a perfect size for a single bite meatball, and follow the cooking time of that recipe. But here are some tips:

* Cut back on cooking time by one-third when cutting the size of a meatball in half. There is not a direct proportion because of half because of the density of most meat mixtures.
* If you want to make a dipping sauce out of a sauce you use for simmering meatballs, add five minutes of cooking time to the meatballs to compensate for the time they would have simmered.
* If you are planning to freeze meatballs, under-cook them by a few minutes so that they will not become too dry when reheated. The reheating should complete the cooking.

Meatballs to Meals

The recipes in this book fall into different categories; some meatballs are meant to be enjoyed as snacks while others are geared to entire meals. A wonderful quality of meatballs is their versatility.

While a meatball sandwich is a tried-and-true favorite, meatballs can also be wrapped in flour tortillas and pita bread. For these types of bread, make the meatballs one inch in diameter.

Meatballs are to spaghetti what chocolate chips are to cookies; they are a natural fit, which is why they are so incredibly popular as combinations. But other carbohydrates and grains are equally good for sopping up a sauce, and many suggestions are given in specific recipes. Couscous, a tiny granular pasta hailing from North Africa, is excellent with Middle Eastern and Mediterranean meatballs; rice is a natural accompaniment for Asian meatballs.

Safety First

The first— and most important— requirement for good cooking, whether the food is a few meatballs or a whole roast, is knowing the basic rules of food safety. This begins with trips to the supermarket and ends after leftovers are refrigerated or frozen at the end of a meal.

The sections that follow may seem like common sense, but after many decades as a food writer I've heard horror stories about very sick people who did not follow basic food safety rules.

If you have any questions about food safety, the U.S. Department of Agriculture is the place to go. The Food Safety Inspection Service was designed to help you. The website, www.fsis.usda.gov, provides a wealth of information in a very user-friendly format.

✳ **Shop Safely:** Most supermarkets are designed to funnel you into the produce section first. But that's not the best place to start. Begin your shopping with the shelf-stable items from the center, then go to produce, and end with the other refrigerated and frozen sections. Never buy meat or poultry in a package that is torn and leaking, and it's a good idea to place all meats and poultry in the disposable plastic bags available in the produce department if not in the meat department. Check the "sell-by" and "use-by" dates, and never purchase food that exceeds them. The case is always stocked with the least fresh on top, so dig down a few layers and you'll probably find packages with more days of life in them. For the trip home, it's a good idea to carry an insulated cooler in the back of your car if it's hot outside or if the perishable items will be out of refrigeration for more than one hour. In hot weather, many seafood departments will provide crushed ice in a separate bag for your fish.

* **Banish Bacteria:** Fruits and vegetables can contain some bacteria, but it's far more likely that the culprits will grow on meat, poultry, and seafood. Store these foods on the bottom shelves of your refrigerator so their juices cannot accidentally drip on other foods. And keep these foods refrigerated until just before they go into the dish. Bacteria multiply at room temperature. The so-called "danger zone" is between 40°F and 140°F. As food cooks, it's important for it to pass through this zone as quickly as possible.

* **Avoid Cross-Contamination:** Cleanliness is not only next to godliness, it's also the key to food safety. Wash your hands often while you're cooking, and never touch cooked food if you haven't washed your hands after handling raw food. The cooked food and raw food shall never meet precept extends beyond the cook's hands. Clean cutting boards, knives, and kitchen counters often. Or if you have the space, section off your countertops for raw foods and cooked foods, as many restaurant kitchens do. Bacteria from raw animal proteins can contaminate the other foods. So don't place cooked foods or raw foods that will remain uncooked (such as salad) on cutting boards that have been used to cut raw meat, poultry, or fish.

* **Choose the Right Cutting Board:** A good way to prevent food-borne illness is by selecting the right cutting board. Wooden boards might be attractive, but you can never get them as clean as plastic boards that can be run through the dishwasher. Even with plastic boards, it's best to use one for only cooked food and foods such as vegetables that are not prone to contain bacteria and another one devoted to raw meats, poultry, and fish.

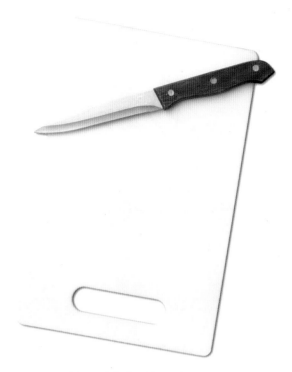

How to Use This Book

All of the recipes are annotated with the number of servings, which is usually given as a range. If the dish is part of a multi-course meal—or if your table will be occupied by eaters with small appetites—the yield can be stretched to feed more people. The recipes for sauces and stocks are given as yields of cups or quarts.

Active time: This is the amount of hands-on prep time needed in the kitchen when you're slicing and dicing.

Start to finish: This is that is the amount of time needed from the moment you start collecting the ingredients to the time you are placing the steaming meatballs on the table. The actual cooking time, as well as any time for chilling, is included in this figure. The unattended time is when you can be reading a book or readying other components of the meal.

Chapter 2

Getting Saucy

*M*any of the individual recipes in this book include a sauce in which the meatballs are cooked or into which they're dipped. But here we're starting with some basic sauces to be used with many of the recipes.

In some recipes I give you an alternative to making a sauce from scratch. To my taste, the Herbed Tomato Sauce has superior flavor to a purchased marinara sauce, but you may not agree. Or you may decide to forego flavor for convenience from time to time. There's no question the supermarket yields a treasure-trove of options for dipping meatballs. Here are some examples:

* Any dip used with a potato or tortilla chip can moisten meatballs, including ranch dip, blue cheese dip, or that old standby onion dip.

* Hummus, the Middle Eastern dip made from chickpeas, comes with many flavors, from roasted garlic to lemon.

* Thick salad dressings such as creamy Italian or Thousand Island work well because they don't drip en route from the bowl to the mouth.

* Barbecue sauces and chutneys can be used straight from the bottle.

* Dry sauce mixes for hollandaise, béarnaise, and brown sauce variations just need to be prepared according to the package instructions.

Herbed Tomato Sauce

Everyone needs a good, basic tomato sauce. Add other herbs, spices, and flavorings as you wish.

Makes 2 cups
Active time: 20 minutes | Start to finish: 1 hour

¼ cup olive oil
1 medium onion, finely chopped
4 garlic cloves, minced
1 carrot, finely chopped
1 celery rib, finely chopped
1 (28-ounce) can crushed tomatoes, undrained
½ cup dry red wine
2 tablespoons chopped fresh parsley
2 tablespoons chopped fresh oregano or 2 teaspoons dried
1 tablespoon fresh thyme or 1 teaspoon dried
2 bay leaves
Salt and freshly ground black pepper to taste

1. Heat olive oil in 2-quart heavy saucepan over medium heat. Add onion and garlic and cook, stirring frequently, for 3 minutes, or until onion is translucent.

2. Add carrot, celery, tomatoes, wine, parsley, oregano, thyme, and bay leaves. Bring to a boil, reduce the heat to low, and simmer sauce, uncovered, stirring occasionally, for 40 minutes, or until lightly thickened. Season to taste with salt and pepper.

Note: The sauce can be refrigerated for up to 4 days, or frozen up to 3 months.

Variation:
✱ Add basil, rosemary, or marjoram along with or instead of some of the herbs listed.

Mexican Tomato Sauce

Makes 2 cups
Active time: 15 minutes | Start to finish: 40 minutes

3 tablespoons olive oil
1 small onion, finely chopped
3 garlic cloves, minced
3 tablespoons chili powder
1 tablespoon ground cumin
1 tablespoon dried oregano
¾ cup chicken stock or vegetable stock
1 (15-ounce) can tomato sauce
1 (4-ounce) can chopped mild green chilies, drained
¼ cup chopped fresh cilantro
Salt and freshly ground black pepper to taste

1. Heat olive oil in a heavy saucepan over medium-high heat. Add onion and garlic and cook, stirring frequently, for 3 minutes, or until the onion is translucent. Reduce the heat to low, stir in the chili powder, cumin, and oregano, and cook, stirring constantly, for 1 minute.

2. Stir in stock, tomato sauce, and green chilies. Whisk well, bring to a boil, and simmer sauce, uncovered, for 15 minutes, stirring occasionally, or until the sauce is reduced by ¼.

3. Stir in cilantro, and season to taste with salt and pepper. Serve hot or at room temperature. The sauce can be refrigerated for up to 4 days, or freeze it for up to 3 months.

Variations:
✱ For a spicier sauce, substitute 2 finely chopped canned chipotle chiles in adobo sauce in place of the green chiles.
✱ Substitute red or white wine for the stock.

Southern Barbecue Sauce

Makes 2 cups
Active time: 10 minutes | *Start to finish: 40 minutes*

1⅓ cups ketchup

½ cup cider vinegar

¼ cup firmly packed dark brown sugar

3 tablespoons Worcestershire sauce

3 tablespoons grated fresh ginger

2 tablespoons vegetable oil

1 tablespoon dry mustard

2 garlic cloves, minced

1 lemon, thinly sliced

½ to 1 teaspoon hot red pepper sauce, or to taste

1. Combine ketchup, vinegar, brown sugar, Worcestershire sauce, ginger, vegetable oil, mustard, garlic, lemon, and red pepper sauce in a saucepan. Bring to a boil over medium heat, stirring occasionally. Reduce the heat to low and simmer sauce, uncovered, for 30 minutes, or until thick, stirring occasionally.

2. Strain sauce, pressing with the back of a spoon to extract as much liquid as possible. Ladle sauce into containers. Refrigerate until ready to use.

Note: The sauce can be refrigerated for up to 2 weeks, or it can be frozen for up to 3 months.

Southwestern Barbecue Sauce

Makes 3 cups
Active time: 15 minutes | *Start to finish: 25 minutes*

2 tablespoons olive oil

1 large onion, chopped

2 garlic cloves, minced

2 canned chipotle chilies in adobo sauce, drained and finely chopped

2 cups crushed tomatoes in tomato puree

½ cup firmly packed dark brown sugar

¼ cup cider vinegar

3 tablespoons freshly squeezed lime juice

2 teaspoons dry mustard

Salt and hot red pepper sauce to taste

1. Heat oil in a saucepan over medium-high heat. Add onion, garlic, and chilies and cook, stirring frequently, for 5 minutes, or until onion softens. Stir in tomatoes, sugar, vinegar, lime juice, and mustard, and bring to a boil over medium heat, stirring frequently.

2. Reduce the heat to low and simmer sauce, uncovered, for 15 minutes. Keep warm.

Note: The sauce can be refrigerated for up to 2 weeks, or frozen up to 3 months.

Asian Dipping Sauce

Makes 2 cups
Active time: 10 minutes | *Start to finish: 10 minutes*

¾ cup unsweetened applesauce

½ cup hoisin sauce

¼ cup firmly packed dark brown sugar

6 tablespoons ketchup

2 tablespoons honey

2 tablespoons rice wine vinegar

1 tablespoon soy sauce

1 tablespoon Chinese chili paste with garlic, or to taste (hot red pepper sauce can be substituted)

Combine applesauce, hoisin sauce, brown sugar, ketchup, honey, vinegar, soy sauce, and chili paste in a mixing bowl. Whisk well, and refrigerate until ready to use. The sauce can be refrigerated up to 1 week.

Ponzu Sauce

Makes 2 cups
Active time: 10 minutes | *Start to finish: 10 minutes*

½ cup soy sauce

½ cup mirin

½ cup freshly squeezed lemon juice

¼ cup Asian sesame oil

3 tablespoons grated fresh ginger

1 tablespoon grated lemon zest

Combine soy sauce, mirin, lemon juice, sesame oil, ginger, and lemon zest in a jar with a tight-fitting lid. Shake well, and refrigerate until ready to use. The sauce can be refrigerated up to 1 week.

Sweet and Sour Sauce

Makes 1½ cups
Active time: 15 minutes | *Start to finish: 20 minutes*

2 tablespoons vegetable oil

4 scallions, white parts and 2-inches of green tops, chopped

2 garlic cloves, minced

2 tablespoons grated fresh ginger

½ cup finely chopped fresh pineapple

½ cup rice vinegar

⅓ cup ketchup

¼ cup firmly packed dark brown sugar

2 tablespoons Chinese chili paste with garlic

1 tablespoon soy sauce

1 tablespoon cornstarch

1. Heat oil in a small saucepan over medium-high heat. Add scallions, garlic, and ginger, and cook, stirring frequently, for 3 minutes, or until scallions are translucent.

2. Add pineapple, vinegar, ketchup, sugar, chili paste, and soy sauce to the pan, and stir well. Bring to a boil over medium-high heat, stirring occasionally. Reduce the heat to low, and simmer sauce, uncovered, for 5 minutes.

3. Combine cornstarch and 1 tablespoon water in a small cup, and stir well. Add mixture to the pan, and cook for 1 minute, or until slightly thickened. Serve sauce at room temperature or chilled.

Note: The sauce can be refrigerated up to 1 week.

Variations:
✳ Substitute mango or papaya for the pineapple.
✳ Omit the chili paste if you want a sauce with no "heat."

Spicy Thai Peanut Sauce

Makes 2 cups
Active time: 10 minutes | *Start to finish: 10 minutes*

1 cup chunky peanut butter

½ cup firmly packed dark brown sugar

⅓ cup freshly squeezed lime juice

¼ cup soy sauce

2 tablespoons Asian sesame oil

2 tablespoons Chinese chili paste with garlic

6 garlic cloves, minced

3 scallions, white parts and 3-inches of green tops, chopped

¼ cup chopped fresh cilantro

Combine peanut butter, ½ cup hot water, brown sugar, lime juice, soy sauce, sesame oil, and chili paste in a mixing bowl. Whisk until well combined. Stir in garlic, scallions, and cilantro. Whisk well again, and refrigerate until ready to use.

Note: The sauce can be refrigerated up to 1 week.

> **Easy with the saltshaker if you're making a dish that also lists soy sauce as an ingredient. Soy sauce is very high in sodium and performs the same function as salt in cooking.**

Thai Sweet and Spicy Dipping Sauce

Makes 2 cups
Active time: 10 minutes | *Start to finish: 10 minutes*

1 cup rice wine vinegar

⅔ cup fish sauce (nam pla)

⅓ cup firmly packed dark brown sugar

6 garlic cloves, minced

1½ teaspoons crushed red pepper flakes, or to taste

Combine vinegar, fish sauce, brown sugar, garlic, and red pepper flakes in a jar with a tight-fitting lid. Shake until sugar is dissolved. Serve at room temperature or chilled. Refrigerate until ready to use.

Note: The sauce can be refrigerated up to 1 week.

Tahini

Makes 2 cups
Active time: 10 minutes | *Start to finish: 10 minutes*

1 cup tahini paste
½ cup freshly squeezed lemon juice
3 garlic cloves, peeled
Salt and cayenne to taste

Combine tahini, ½ cup water, lemon juice, garlic, salt, and cayenne in a blender. Blend until smooth, scraping the inside of the jar as necessary. Refrigerate until ready to use.

Note: The sauce can be refrigerated for up to 4 days.

Scallion Dill Sauce

Makes 2 cups
Active time: 10 minutes | *Start to finish: 10 minutes*

1 cup sour cream
¾ cup mayonnaise
¼ cup freshly squeezed lemon juice
⅓ cup finely chopped scallions, white parts and 3 inches of green tops
¼ cup chopped fresh dill or 2 tablespoons dried
2 garlic cloves, minced
Salt and freshly ground black pepper to taste

Whisk sour cream, mayonnaise, and lemon juice together until smooth. Stir in scallions, dill, and garlic. Season to taste with salt and pepper. Refrigerate until ready to use.

Note: The sauce can be refrigerated for up to 4 days.

Variation:
✽ For a low-fat version, substitute non-fat yogurt for both the mayonnaise and sour cream.

Creamy Chipotle Sauce

Makes 2 cups
Active time: 10 minutes | *Start to finish: 10 minutes*

1 cup mayonnaise
⅔ cup sour cream
3 tablespoons freshly squeezed lime juice
3 scallions, white parts and 3-inches of green tops, chopped
3 garlic cloves, minced
3 chipotle chiles in adobo sauce, finely chopped
1 teaspoon adobo sauce
Salt to taste

Combine mayonnaise, sour cream, lime juice, scallions, garlic, chiles, and adobo sauce in a mixing bowl. Whisk well, and season to taste with salt. Refrigerate until ready to use.

Note: The sauce can be refrigerated for up to 4 days.

Variation:
✽ To make a low-fat version, substitute non-fat yogurt for both the mayonnaise and sour cream.

Blue Cheese Sauce

Makes 2 cups
Active time: 10 minutes | *Start to finish: 10 minutes*

¾ cup mayonnaise

½ cup sour cream

2 tablespoons white wine vinegar

½ pound blue cheese, crumbled

3 tablespoons chopped fresh chives

Salt and freshly ground black pepper to taste

Whisk mayonnaise, sour cream, and vinegar together until smooth. Stir in blue cheese and chives, and season to taste with salt and pepper.

Note: The sauce can be refrigerated for up to 4 days.

Variations:
* For a low-fat version, substitute non-fat yogurt for both the mayonnaise and sour cream.
* Finely chopped scallion tops can be substituted in this or in any recipe in place of chives. Don't use the white part of the scallions; they're too strong.

Greek Feta Sauce

Makes 1½ cups
Active time: 10 minutes | *Start to finish: 10 minutes*

½ pound mild feta cheese, diced

½ cup sour cream

¼ cup plain whole milk yogurt, preferably Greek

¼ cup olive oil

2 tablespoons freshly squeezed lemon juice

2 garlic cloves, peeled

¼ cup chopped fresh dill or 2 tablespoons dried

Salt and freshly ground black pepper to taste

Combine feta, sour cream, yogurt, olive oil, lemon juice, and garlic in a food processor fitted with a steel blade or in a blender. Puree until smooth. Scrape mixture into a mixing bowl, and stir in dill. Whisk well, and season to taste with salt and pepper. Refrigerate until ready to use.

Note: The sauce can be refrigerated for up to 4 days.

Variation:
* To make a low-fat version, substitute more yogurt for the sour cream.

Easy Aïoli

Makes 2 cups
Active time: 10 minutes | *Start to finish: 10 minutes*

1½ cups mayonnaise

6 garlic cloves, minced

3 tablespoons freshly squeezed lemon juice

2 tablespoons smooth Dijon mustard

Salt and freshly ground black pepper to taste

Combine mayonnaise, garlic, lemon juice, and mustard in a mixing bowl. Whisk well, and season to taste with salt and pepper. Refrigerate until ready to use.

Note: The sauce can be refrigerated for up to 4 days.

Variations:
* Add 2 tablespoons chili powder.
* Add ¼ cup pureed roasted red bell peppers.

Remoulade

Makes 2 cups
Active time: 10 minutes | *Start to finish: 10 minutes*

1⅓ cups mayonnaise

6 scallions, white parts and 2-inches of green tops, chopped

3 garlic cloves, minced

¼ cup freshly squeezed lemon juice

3 tablespoons grainy mustard

3 tablespoons chopped fresh parsley

3 tablespoons prepared white horseradish

2 tablespoons bottled chili sauce

Salt and freshly ground black pepper to taste

Combine mayonnaise, scallions, garlic, lemon juice, mustard, parsley, horseradish, and chili sauce in a mixing bowl. Whisk well, and season to taste with salt and pepper. Refrigerate until ready to use.

Note: The sauce can be refrigerated for up to 4 days.

Variations:
* Add 1 or 2 grated hard-boiled eggs.
* Add 2 tablespoons Worcestershire sauce.

Cucumber Raita

Makes 2 cups
Active time: 10 minutes | *Start to finish: 10 minutes*

½ medium cucumber, finely chopped

2 ripe plum tomatoes, cored, seeded, and finely chopped

2 scallions, white parts and 3-inches of green tops, finely chopped

2 garlic cloves, minced

1 cup plain yogurt

2 tablespoons chopped fresh dill or 2 teaspoons dried

2 tablespoons freshly squeezed lemon juice

Salt and freshly ground black pepper to taste

Combine cucumber, tomatoes, scallions, garlic, yogurt, dill, and lemon juice in a mixing bowl. Whisk well, and season to taste with salt and pepper. Refrigerate until ready to use.

Note: The sauce can be refrigerated for up to 4 days.

Variations:

* Add 1 tablespoon ground cumin and 2 teaspoons ground coriander.
* Substitute 3 tablespoons chopped fresh oregano for the dill.

Middle Eastern Yogurt Sauce

Makes 2 cups
Active time: 10 minutes | *Start to finish: 40 minutes*

2 cups plain yogurt

2 scallions, white parts only, chopped

3 garlic cloves, minced

2 tablespoons finely chopped fresh mint

1 tablespoon olive oil

Salt and freshly ground black pepper to taste

1. Place yogurt in a fine-meshed sieve over a mixing bowl, and allow it to drain for 30 minutes at room temperature, or up to 4 hours refrigerated.

2. Discard whey from the mixing bowl, and return yogurt to the bowl. Add scallions, garlic, mint, and olive oil. Whisk well, and season to taste with salt and pepper. Refrigerate until ready to use.

Note: The sauce can be refrigerated for up to 4 days.

Variations:

* Add ¼ cup very finely chopped tomato.
* Substitute fresh chopped oregano for the mint.

Sesame Honey Mustard Sauce

Makes 2 cups
Active time: 10 minutes | *Start to finish: 10 minutes*

1 cup Dijon mustard

⅔ cup honey

⅓ cup Asian sesame oil

½ cup chopped fresh cilantro

Salt and freshly ground black pepper to taste

Combine mustard, honey, sesame oil, and cilantro in a mixing bowl. Whisk well, and season to taste with salt and pepper. Refrigerate until ready to use.

Note: The sauce can be refrigerated for up to 1 week.

Tartar Sauce

Makes 2 cups
Active time: 10 minutes | *Start to finish: 10 minutes*

1½ cups mayonnaise

3 scallions, white parts only, chopped

¼ cup finely chopped cornichons

3 tablespoons small capers, drained and rinsed

2 tablespoons white wine vinegar

2 tablespoons chopped fresh parsley

1 tablespoon smooth Dijon mustard

1 tablespoon chopped fresh tarragon or 1 teaspoon dried

Salt and freshly ground black pepper to taste

Combine mayonnaise, scallions, cornichons, capers, vinegar, parsley, mustard and tarragon in a mixing bowl. Whisk well, and season to taste with salt and pepper. Refrigerate until ready to use.

Note: The sauce can be refrigerated for up to 4 days.

Chapter 3

Now That's a Meatball:

International Beef Meatballs

$\mathcal{M}$eatballs from ground beef are an essential part of every American cook's repertoire; a meatball recipe was probably the first dish many learned to cook. During my childhood beef was the only ground meat found in the supermarket except for sausage, so occasionally those two would be combined. While that is hardly the case today, and later chapters feature recipes for everything from pork and veal to lamb and poultry, the star of the recipes in this chapter is beef.

Economy enjoying beef in its ground form is one of the most economical ways to serve it. While chuck roasts and other cuts for pot roasts and stews cost about the same as ground chuck, they take far longer to cook. Almost all of the recipes in this chapter can be on the table in less than one hour; that's about one-third the time it takes to produce a stew or braised dish.

Again, returning to the memories of my childhood, ground beef was pretty much the only option. Today's meat case is filled with a dizzying array of packages with various fat contents and ground from various parts of the cow. My choice is always ground chuck, which is used in these recipes because it has the best beefy flavor and is reasonably priced. While you can spend far more on ground sirloin, I don't think it has the inherent taste of ground chuck.

Herbed Italian Beef Meatballs

A combination of different herbs, various vegetables, and two cheeses give these easy meatballs tremendous flavor. They make a great hors d'oeuvre, or you can keep them in the freezer to use on pizza or to top spaghetti.

Makes 4 to 6 servings | *Active time: 20 minutes* | *Start to finish: 35 minutes*

3 slices white bread

3 tablespoons whole milk

3 tablespoons olive oil

1 small onion, finely chopped

2 garlic cloves, minced

1 small carrot, grated

1 large egg

3 tablespoons chopped fresh parsley

2 tablespoons chopped fresh basil
or 2 teaspoons dried

1 tablespoon chopped fresh oregano
or 1 teaspoon dried

½ cup grated whole milk mozzarella

¼ cup freshly grated Parmesan

1¼ pounds ground chuck

Salt and freshly ground black pepper
to taste

Chopped fresh parsley, for garnish,
if desired

Vegetable oil spray

FOR DIPPING:

1 cup Herbed Tomato Sauce (page 21)
or any purchased marinara sauce, heated

1. Preheat the oven to 450°F. Line a rimmed baking sheet with heavy-duty aluminum foil, and spray the foil with vegetable oil spray. Tear bread into small pieces, and place bread in a bowl with milk; stir well.

2. Heat oil in a small skillet over medium-high heat. Add onion, garlic, and carrot, and cook, stirring frequently, for 3 minutes, or until onion is translucent. While vegetables cook, whisk egg in a mixing bowl, and add bread mixture, parsley, basil, oregano, mozzarella, and Parmesan, and mix well.

3. Add onion mixture and beef to the mixing bowl, season to taste with salt and pepper, and mix well again. Make mixture into 1½-inch meatballs, and arrange meatballs on the prepared pan. Spray tops of meatballs with vegetable oil spray.

4. Bake meatballs for 12 to 15 minutes, or until cooked through. Remove the pan from the oven, and serve immediately, accompanied by a bowl of Herbed Tomato Sauce for dipping. Garnish with parsley, if desired.

Note: The beef mixture can be prepared up to 1 day in advance and refrigerated, tightly covered. Also, the meatballs can be baked up to 2 days in advance and refrigerated, tightly covered. Reheat them in a 350°F oven, covered, for 10 to 12 minutes, or until hot.

Variations:

✳ Make the meatballs with a combination of ground beef, ground pork, and Italian sausage.

✳ Make the meatballs with ground turkey.

A great way to grate cheese, especially hard cheeses like Parmesan, is in a food processor. If grating cheese by hand with a box grater, spray some vegetable oil spray on the blades and the cheese will be easier to grate.

Blue Cheese Beef Meatballs

Blue cheese is a natural pairing with hearty beef. Dip these meatballs in a blue cheese sauce to add moisture and reinforce the sharp cheesy flavor.

Makes 4 to 6 servings | Active time: 15 minutes | Start to finish: 30 minutes

3 slices white bread

⅓ cup whole milk

2 tablespoons unsalted butter

1 small onion, finely chopped

2 garlic cloves, minced

1 large egg

2 tablespoons chopped fresh parsley

¾ cup crumbled blue cheese

1 tablespoon fresh thyme
or 1 teaspoon dried

1¼ pounds ground chuck

Salt and freshly ground black pepper
to taste

Vegetable oil spray

FOR DIPPING:

1 cup Blue Cheese Sauce (page 29)
or purchased blue cheese dressing

1. Preheat the oven to 450°F. Line a rimmed baking sheet with heavy-duty aluminum foil, and spray the foil with vegetable oil spray. Tear bread into small pieces, and place bread in a bowl with milk; stir well.

2. Heat butter in a small skillet over medium-high heat. Add onion and garlic, and cook, stirring frequently, for 3 minutes, or until onion is translucent. While vegetables cook, whisk egg in a mixing bowl, and add bread mixture, parsley, cheese, and thyme, and mix well.

3. Add onion mixture and beef to the mixing bowl, season to taste with salt and pepper, and mix well again. Make mixture into 1½-inch meatballs, and arrange meatballs on the prepared pan. Spray tops of meatballs with vegetable oil spray.

4. Bake meatballs for 12 to 15 minutes, or until cooked through. Remove the pan from the oven, and serve immediately, accompanied by a bowl of Blue Cheese Sauce for dipping.

Note: The beef mixture can be prepared up to 1 day in advance and refrigerated, tightly covered. Also, the meatballs can be baked up to 2 days in advance and refrigerated, tightly covered. Reheat them in a 350°F oven, covered, for 10 to 12 minutes, or until hot.

Variations:
* Ground turkey can be substituted for the beef. Cook turkey to an internal temperature of 160°F on an instant-read thermometer or until cooked through and no longer pink.
* Also, any blue-veined cheese—from Italian Gorgonzola to English stilton—works well in this recipe.

Peppery Mustard Beef Shooters

A touch of heady red wine, some herbs, and piquant capers flavor these hearty beef meatballs that are similar in flavor to the classic French steak au poivre. Just put them out with additional Dijon mustard for dipping.

Makes about 12 shooters or 4 to 6 servings | *Active time: 15 minutes* | *Start to finish: 30 minutes*

1 large egg

¼ cup dry red wine

½ cup plain breadcrumbs, divided

2 tablespoons grainy Dijon mustard

2 shallots, finely chopped

2 garlic cloves, minced

2 tablespoons small capers, drained, rinsed, and chopped

1 tablespoon fresh thyme
or 1 teaspoon dried

1¼ pounds ground chuck

Salt to taste

3 tablespoons coarsely ground mixed peppercorns

Vegetable oil spray

FOR DIPPING:

½ cup Dijon mustard

¼ cup mayonnaise

Mustard sprouts for garnish

1. Preheat the oven to 450°F. Line a rimmed baking sheet with heavy-duty aluminum foil, and spray the foil with vegetable oil spray.

2. Combine egg and wine in a mixing bowl, and whisk well. Add ¼ cup breadcrumbs, mustard, shallots, garlic, capers, and thyme, and mix well. Add beef, season to taste with salt, and mix well again.

3. Combine remaining ¼ cup breadcrumbs and pepper in a small bowl. Make mixture into 1½-inch meatballs, and roll meatballs in pepper mixture. Arrange meatballs on the prepared pan, and spray tops of meatballs with vegetable oil spray.

4. Bake meatballs for 12 to 15 minutes, or until cooked through. While meatballs are cooking, combine mustard and mayonnaise. Spoon some of the mixture into a dozen tall glasses and top with mustard sprouts. When meatballs are done, skewer with toothpicks and place on top of the glasses.

Note: The beef mixture can be prepared up to 1 day in advance and refrigerated, tightly covered. Also, the meatballs can be baked up to 2 days in advance and refrigerated, tightly covered. Reheat them in a 350°F oven, covered, for 10 to 12 minutes or until hot.

Variation:

✳ Use lamb in place of the beef; omit the capers and add 2 tablespoons chopped fresh rosemary (or 2 teaspoons dried rosemary) to the meat mixture.

Shepherd's Pie with Meatballs and Cheddar-Mashed Potatoes

Flavorful meatballs in a rich brown gravy with vegetables are crowned with a layer of cheddar-flavored mashed potatoes in this all-in-one dinner.

Makes 6 to 8 servings | *Active time: 25 minutes* | *Start to finish: 1¼ hours*

2 pounds red potatoes, scrubbed and cut into 1-inch dice

½ cup heavy cream

4 tablespoons unsalted butter

1½ cups grated sharp cheddar, divided

Salt and freshly ground black pepper to taste

¼ cup olive oil

1 large onion, finely chopped

2 garlic cloves, minced

¼ pound fresh mushrooms, chopped

1 large egg

2 tablespoons whole milk

½ cup plain breadcrumbs

1½ pounds ground chuck

2 cups dry red wine

1 (1.1-ounce) package mushroom gravy mix

2 tablespoons chopped fresh parsley

1 tablespoon fresh thyme or 1 teaspoon dried

1 (10-ounce) package frozen mixed vegetables, thawed

1. Place potatoes in a saucepan of salted water, and bring to a boil over high heat. Reduce the heat to medium, and cook potatoes, uncovered, for 10 to 15 minutes, or until tender when pierced with the tip of a paring knife. Drain potatoes. Heat cream, butter, and 1 cup cheese in the saucepan over medium heat until cheese melts, stirring occasionally. Return potatoes to saucepan, and mash well with a potato masher. Season to taste with salt and pepper, and set aside.

2. Preheat the oven broiler. Line a rimmed baking sheet with heavy-duty aluminum foil, and spray the foil with vegetable oil spray.

3. Heat oil in a large skillet over medium-high heat. Add onion and garlic, and cook, stirring frequently, for 3 minutes, or until onion is translucent. Add mushrooms, and cook an additional 3 minutes, stirring frequently. While vegetables cook, whisk egg and milk in a mixing bowl, add breadcrumbs, and mix well.

4. Add onion mixture and beef to the mixing bowl, season to taste with salt and pepper, and mix well again. Make mixture into 1½-inch meatballs, and arrange meatballs on the prepared pan. Spray tops of meatballs with vegetable oil spray.

5. Broil meatballs 6-inches from the broiler element, turning them with tongs to brown all sides. Remove meatballs from baking pan with a slotted spoon, and set aside.

6. Combine wine, gravy mix, parsley, and thyme in a saucepan, and whisk well. Bring to a boil over medium-high heat, whisking frequently, and simmer over low heat for 2 minutes.

7. Preheat the oven to 400°F, and grease a 9 x 13-inch baking pan. Arrange meatballs in the pan, and pour sauce over them. Cover the pan with heavy-duty aluminum foil, and bake for 15 minutes. Stir in the mixed vegetables, and bake an additional 10 minutes.

8. Increase the oven temperature to 450°F. Spread potato mixture on top of meatballs, and sprinkle with remaining ½ cup cheese. Bake for 15 minutes, or until top is golden. Serve immediately.

Wild Mushroom and Caramelized Onion Beef Meatballs

Between the sweet brown onions, the woodsy mushrooms, and the heady cheese there is so much flavor in these meatballs that they need no additional sauce for dipping or topping. Serve them with mashed potatoes and a green salad.

Makes 4 to 6 servings | *Active time: 30 minutes* | *Start to finish: 45 minutes*

3 tablespoons olive oil

2 tablespoons (¼ stick) unsalted butter

2 large onions, diced

Salt and freshly ground black pepper to taste

2 teaspoons granulated sugar

½ pound fresh shiitake mushrooms

2 garlic cloves, minced

1 large egg

½ cup plain breadcrumbs

3 tablespoons whole milk

½ cup grated Gruyère

2 teaspoons fresh thyme or 1 teaspoon dried

1¼ pounds ground chuck

Vegetable oil spray

1. Heat oil and butter in a large skillet over medium heat. Add onions, and toss to coat. Cover the pan, and cook onions for 10 minutes, stirring occasionally. Sprinkle onions with salt, pepper, and sugar, and raise the heat to medium-high. Cook onions for 10 to 15 minutes, or until brown.

2. While onions cook, wipe mushrooms with a damp paper towel, discard stems, and chop finely. Preheat the oven to 450°F. Line a rimmed baking sheet with heavy-duty aluminum foil, and spray the foil with vegetable oil spray.

3. Add mushrooms and garlic to the skillet, and cook, stirring frequently, for 5 to 7 minutes or until mushrooms are soft.

4. Combine egg, breadcrumbs, milk, cheese, and thyme in a mixing bowl, and mix well. Add beef and vegetables, season to taste with salt and pepper, and mix well again. Make mixture into 1½-inch meatballs, and arrange meatballs on the prepared pan. Spray tops of meatballs with vegetable oil spray.

5. Bake meatballs for 12 to 15 minutes, or until cooked through. Remove the pan from the oven, and serve immediately.

Note: The beef mixture can be prepared up to 1 day in advance and refrigerated, tightly covered. Also, the meatballs can be baked up to 2 days in advance and refrigerated, tightly covered. Reheat them in a 350°F oven, covered, for 10 to 12 minutes, or until hot.

Variation:

* Ground lamb can be substituted for the beef.

The process of cooking vegetables covered over low heat is called "sweating," although it has nothing to do with exercise. The purpose of this initial covered cooking is to soften the vegetables without letting it brown; this facilitates the browning later on.

Mustard-Dill Beef Meatballs

Many Scandinavian dishes feature aromatic dill. The freshness of the dill is a nice balance with the sharpness of the mustard.

Makes 4 to 6 servings | Active time: 15 minutes | Start to finish: 30 minutes

2 tablespoons unsalted butter

1 small onion, chopped

2 garlic cloves, minced

½ cup beef stock

1 large egg

2 tablespoons Dijon mustard

3 slices seeded rye bread

¼ cup chopped fresh dill

1¼ pounds ground chuck

Salt and freshly ground black pepper to taste

Vegetable oil spray

FOR DIPPING:

1 cup Scallion Dill Sauce (page 27)

1. Preheat the oven to 450°F. Line a rimmed baking sheet with heavy-duty aluminum foil, and spray the foil with vegetable oil spray.

2. Heat butter in a small skillet over medium-high heat. Add onion and garlic and cook, stirring frequently, for 3 minutes, or until onion is translucent. While vegetables cook, combine stock, egg, and mustard in a mixing bowl, and whisk until smooth. Tear bread into small pieces, and add to the bowl, along with dill, and mix well.

3. Add shallot mixture and beef, season to taste with salt and pepper, and mix well again. Make mixture into 1½-inch meatballs, and arrange meatballs on the prepared pan. Spray tops of meatballs with vegetable oil spray.

4. Bake meatballs for 12 to 15 minutes, or until cooked through. Remove from the oven. Serve with Scallion Dill Sauce on the meatballs or on the side for dipping.

Note: The beef mixture can be prepared up to 1 day in advance and refrigerated, tightly covered. Also, the meatballs can be baked up to 2 days in advance and refrigerated, tightly covered. Reheat them in a 350°F oven, covered, for 10 to 12 minutes, or until hot.

Variation:

✳ For a lighter dish, replace the beef with ground turkey or ground pork.

The word "dill" comes from the Norse *dilla*, meaning to lull. Drinking dill tea was used to cure insomnia. The ancient Greeks and Romans knew dill as a medicinal herb; soldiers placed burned dill seeds on their wounds to promote healing.

Provençal Beef Meatballs with Red Wine Sauce

Think of this dish as a meatball version of the classic French boeuf bourguignon; the meatballs are cooked in a mixture of red wine and herbs. Serve the meatballs over buttered egg noodles or mashed potatoes and accompanied with a Burgundy wine. In a dish such as this one in which the meatballs are merely browned but not cooked through initially, the dish must be cooked to completion before refrigerating. The partially cooked meatballs contain raw egg, and can cause illness.

Makes 4 to 6 servings | *Active time: 20 minutes* | *Start to finish: 1¼ hours*

3 tablespoons unsalted butter

1 medium onion, chopped

2 garlic cloves, minced

1 large egg

¼ cup whole milk

½ cup plain breadcrumbs

3 tablespoons chopped fresh parsley

1 tablespoon fresh thyme or 1 teaspoon dried

1¼ pounds ground chuck

Salt and freshly ground black pepper to taste

Vegetable oil spray

1¼ cups dry red wine

1 cup beef stock

3 tablespoons tomato paste

1 tablespoon herbes de Provence

1 cup grated Gruyère

1. Preheat the oven broiler. Line a rimmed baking sheet with heavy-duty aluminum foil, and spray the foil with vegetable oil spray.

2. Heat butter in a small skillet over medium-high heat. Add onion and garlic and cook, stirring frequently, for 3 minutes, or until onion is translucent. While vegetables cook, combine egg and milk in a mixing bowl, and whisk until smooth. Add breadcrumbs, parsley, and thyme, and mix well.

3. Add onion mixture and beef, season to taste with salt and pepper, and mix well again. Make mixture into 2-inch meatballs, and arrange meatballs on the prepared pan. Spray tops of meatballs with vegetable oil spray.

4. Broil meatballs 6-inches from the broiler element, turning them with tongs to brown all sides. Remove meatballs from the broiler, and transfer to a 9 x 13-inch pan. Preheat the oven to 375°F.

5. Whisk wine, stock, and tomato paste in a mixing bowl, and season to taste with salt and pepper. Pour mixture over meatballs. Cover the pan with aluminum foil, and bake for 30 minutes. Remove the pan from the oven, sprinkle cheese on top, and bake for an additional 15 minutes, or until cheese is melted and bubbly. Serve immediately.

Note: The meatball mixture can be prepared up to 1 day in advance and refrigerated, tightly covered. Also, the dish can be cooked up to 2 days in advance and refrigerated, tightly covered. Reheat in a 350°F oven, covered, for 15 to 20 minutes, or until hot.

Variations:

✳ Add ½ pound sautéed sliced mushrooms to the sauce.

✳ Cut red potatoes into 1-inch cubes, and bake them in the dish along with the meatballs and sauce.

Scandinavian Beef Meatballs in Sour-Cherry Sauce

Northern European cuisines, such as those from the Scandinavian countries as well as Germany and Austria, frequently use fruit in savory dishes, like the dried cherries here. Serve these meatballs with roasted potatoes and baby spinach. If you have trouble finding dried sour cherries, use dried sweet cherries or dried cranberries. Add two tablespoons of freshly squeezed lemon juice to the sauce to compensate.

Makes 4 to 6 servings | Active time: 25 minutes | Start to finish: 50 minutes

1½ cups dried sour cherries
2 cups beef stock, divided
¼ cup olive oil
2 medium onions, chopped
1 small carrot, chopped
1 large egg
½ cup plain breadcrumbs
2 garlic cloves, minced
¾ teaspoon ground cinnamon
½ teaspoon ground ginger
Pinch of ground allspice
1¼ pounds ground chuck
Salt and freshly ground black pepper to taste
1 tablespoon cornstarch
1 tablespoon kirsch
Vegetable oil spray

1. Combine dried cherries and 1¾ cups beef stock in a saucepan, and bring to a boil over medium-high heat. Remove the pan from the heat, and allow cherries to soak. Heat oil in a large skillet over medium-high heat, add onions and carrot, and cook, stirring frequently, for 3 minutes, or until onions are translucent. Add cherries and stock, bring to a boil, and simmer sauce, covered, for 15 minutes.

2. While sauce simmers, preheat the oven broiler. Line a rimmed baking sheet with heavy-duty aluminum foil, and spray the foil with vegetable oil spray.

3. Combine egg and remaining ¼ cup stock in a mixing bowl, and whisk until smooth. Add breadcrumbs, garlic, cinnamon, ginger, and allspice, and mix well. Add beef, season to taste with salt and pepper, and mix well again. Make mixture into 1½-inch meatballs, and arrange meatballs on the prepared pan. Spray tops of meatballs with vegetable oil spray.

4. Broil meatballs 6 inches from the broiler element, turning them with tongs to brown all sides. Remove meatballs from baking pan with a slotted spoon, and add meatballs to sauce. Bring to a boil, and simmer meatballs, covered, over low heat, turning occasionally with a slotted spoon, for 15 minutes.

5. Combine cornstarch and kirsch in a small bowl, and stir well. Add mixture to sauce, and simmer, uncovered, for 2 minutes, or until slightly thickened. Serve immediately.

Note: The meatball mixture can be prepared up to 1 day in advance and refrigerated, tightly covered. Also, the dish can be cooked up to 2 days in advance and refrigerated, tightly covered. Reheat in a 350°F oven, covered, for 15 to 20 minutes, or until hot.

Variation:
✳ Make the meatballs from a combination of ground pork and ground beef; it will be lighter and the fruit flavor will seem more intense.

Beef Meatball Hungarian Goulash

Goulash is the native stew of Hungary, and almost all meats end up cooked this flavorful way. Serve these meatballs over some buttered egg noodles with a steamed green vegetable for a contrasting color and flavor.

Makes 4 to 6 servings | Active time: 25 minutes | Start to finish: 45 minutes

2 tablespoons olive oil

2 large onions, chopped

3 garlic cloves, minced

1 large egg

2 tablespoons whole milk

2 slices seeded rye bread

1¼ pounds ground chuck

Salt and freshly ground black pepper to taste

5 tablespoons paprika, preferably Hungarian

2 tablespoons tomato paste

2 cups Beef Stock (page 197) or purchased beef stock

2 teaspoons crushed caraway seeds

¾ cup sour cream (optional)

Vegetable oil spray

1. Preheat the oven broiler. Line a rimmed baking sheet with heavy-duty aluminum foil, and spray the foil with vegetable oil spray.

2. Heat oil in a skillet over medium-high heat. Add onion and garlic and cook, stirring frequently, for 3 minutes, or until onion is translucent. While vegetables cook, combine egg and milk in a mixing bowl, and whisk until smooth. Break bread into tiny pieces and add to mixing bowl, and mix well.

3. Add ½ of onion mixture and beef, season to taste with salt and pepper, and mix well again. Make mixture into 2-inch meatballs, and arrange meatballs on the prepared pan. Spray tops of meatballs with vegetable oil spray.

4. Broil meatballs 6-inches from the broiler element, turning them with tongs to brown all sides. While meatballs brown, add paprika to the skillet containing remaining onions and garlic. Cook over low heat for 1 minute, stirring constantly. Add tomato paste, stock, and caraway seeds, and whisk well. Bring to a boil over medium-high heat, stirring occasionally.

5. Remove meatballs from the baking pan with a slotted spoon, and add meatballs to sauce. Bring to a boil, and simmer the meatballs, covered, over low heat, turning occasionally with a slotted spoon, for 15 minutes. Stir in sour cream, if desired, and serve immediately. *Do not allow sauce to boil.*

Note: The meatball mixture can be prepared up to 1 day in advance and refrigerated, tightly covered. Also, the dish can be cooked up to 2 days in advance and refrigerated, tightly covered. Reheat in a 350°F oven, covered, for 15 to 20 minutes, or until hot.

Variation:

❋ Make the meatballs from ground turkey or ground pork.

Paprika is a powder made by grinding aromatic sweet red pepper pods several times. The color can vary from deep red to bright orange, and the flavor ranges from mild to pungent and hot. Hungarian cuisine is characterized by paprika as a flavoring, and Hungarian paprika is considered the best.

Southwestern Barbecued Beef Meatballs

These easy-to-make meatballs contain a wide range of popular Southwestern flavors— from fiery chiles to creamy cheese and lots of herbs and spices. Serve them with a basket of warm flour tortillas for making burritos.

Makes 4 to 6 servings | *Active time: 20 minutes* | *Start to finish: 35 minutes*

1 large egg

2 chipotle chiles in adobo sauce

2 tablespoons whole milk

½ cup plain breadcrumbs

½ cup grated jalapeño Jack cheese

3 tablespoons chopped fresh cilantro

3 tablespoons diced canned mild green chiles, drained

4 garlic cloves, minced

1 tablespoon dried oregano

1 tablespoon Spanish smoked paprika

2 teaspoons ground cumin

1¼ pounds ground chuck

Salt and freshly ground black pepper to taste

Vegetable oil spray

FOR DIPPING:

1 cup Southwestern Barbecue Sauce (page 23) or bottled salsa, heated

1. Preheat the oven to 450°F. Line a rimmed baking sheet with heavy-duty aluminum foil, and spray the foil with vegetable oil spray.

2. Combine egg, chipotle chilies, milk, and breadcrumbs in a food processor or in a blender, and puree until smooth. Scrape mixture into a mixing bowl. Add cheese, cilantro, green chilies, garlic, oregano, paprika, and cumin, and mix well.

3. Add beef, season to taste with salt and pepper, and mix well again. Make mixture into 1½-inch meatballs, and arrange meatballs on the prepared pan. Spray tops of meatballs with vegetable oil spray.

4. Bake meatballs for 12 to 15 minutes, or until cooked through. Remove the pan from the oven, and serve immediately accompanied by a bowl of Southwestern Barbecue Sauce for dipping.

Note: The meatball mixture can be prepared up to 1 day in advance and refrigerated, tightly covered. Also, the dish can be cooked up to 2 days in advance and refrigerated, tightly covered. Reheat in a 350°F oven, covered, for 15 to 20 minutes, or until hot.

Variations:

✱ Make lighter meatballs by using ground turkey in place of the beef.

✱ Adjust the spiciness by using plain Monterey Jack cheese rather than the jalapeño version and serving with a mild barbecue sauce, such as the Southern Barbecue Sauce (page 23).

Those small cans of chilies can look a lot alike, especially when you're in a hurry. Make sure you buy the mild green chiles, not diced jalapeño peppers. You'd be in for a surprise.

Spicy Mexican Smoked Cheddar-Beef Meatballs

The bacon adds a smoky nuance to these spicy meatballs, which are delicious, served with Mexican rice or saffron rice and some sautéed zucchini. And beer is the best beverage to accompany them.

Makes 4 to 6 servings | *Active time: 25 minutes* | *Start to finish: 40 minutes*

¼ pound bacon, cut into thin slivers

1 medium onion, chopped

3 garlic cloves, minced

2 large jalapeño or serrano chiles, seeds and ribs removed, and finely chopped

1 large egg

¼ cup whole milk

½ cup plain breadcrumbs

½ cup grated smoked cheddar

2 tablespoons chopped fresh cilantro

1 tablespoon dried oregano

2 teaspoons ground cumin

1¼ pounds ground chuck

Salt and freshly ground black pepper to taste

Vegetable oil spray

FOR DIPPING:

1 cup Mexican Tomato Sauce (page 21), heated

1. Preheat the oven to 450°F. Line a rimmed baking sheet with heavy-duty aluminum foil, and spray the foil with vegetable oil spray.

2. Place bacon in a large skillet over medium-high heat. Cook, stirring occasionally, until bacon is crisp. Remove bacon from the pan with a slotted spoon, and set aside. Discard all but 2 tablespoons bacon fat from the skillet.

3. Add onion, garlic, and chiles to the skillet and cook, stirring frequently, for 3 minutes, or until onion is translucent. While vegetables cook, combine egg and milk in a mixing bowl, and whisk until smooth. Add breadcrumbs, cheddar, cilantro, oregano, and cumin, and mix well.

4. Add onion mixture, bacon, and beef, season to taste with salt and pepper, and mix well again. Make mixture into 1½-inch meatballs, and arrange meatballs on the prepared pan. Spray tops of meatballs with vegetable oil spray.

5. Bake meatballs for 12 to 15 minutes, or until cooked through. Remove the pan from the oven, and serve immediately accompanied by a bowl of Mexican Tomato Sauce for dipping.

Note: The beef mixture can be prepared up to 1 day in advance and refrigerated, tightly covered. Also, the meatballs can be baked up to 2 days in advance and refrigerated, tightly covered. Reheat them in a 350°F oven, covered, for 10 to 12 minutes, or until hot.

Variation:

✳ Use a combination of ground pork and ground veal for a lighter flavor.

As a general rule, the smaller the chile pepper, the hotter the chile pepper. That's why an equal number is given for tiny serrano and much larger jalapeño peppers. And another generality is that most of the "heat" is in the seeds and ribs, which is why you are most often instructed to remove them.

Moroccan Beef Meatballs with Tomato Sauce

Aromatic cinnamon and earthy cumin are the dominant flavors in these Moroccan-inspired meatballs. Serve them over couscous to enjoy every drop of sauce.

Makes 4 to 6 servings | Active time: 20 minutes | Start to finish: 45 minutes

¼ cup olive oil

2 large onions, chopped

4 garlic cloves, minced

1 large egg

2 tablespoons whole milk

½ cup panko breadcrumbs

⅔ cup chopped fresh parsley, divided

1 tablespoon chili powder

½ teaspoon ground cinnamon

1¼ pounds ground chuck

Salt and cayenne to taste

2 (8-ounce) cans tomato sauce

2 teaspoons ground cumin

Freshly ground black pepper to taste

Fresh thyme for garnish, if desired

Vegetable oil spray

1. Preheat the oven broiler. Line a rimmed baking sheet with heavy-duty aluminum foil, and spray the foil with vegetable oil spray.

2. Heat oil in a skillet over medium-high heat. Add onion and garlic and cook, stirring frequently, for 3 minutes, or until onion is translucent. While vegetables cook, combine egg and milk in a mixing bowl, and whisk until smooth. Add breadcrumbs, ⅓ cup parsley, chili powder, and cinnamon, and mix well.

3. Add ½ of onion mixture and beef, season to taste with salt and cayenne, and mix well again. Make mixture into 2-inch meatballs, and arrange meatballs on the prepared pan. Spray tops of meatballs with vegetable oil spray.

4. Broil meatballs 6-inches from the broiler element, turning them with tongs to brown all sides. While meatballs brown, add tomato sauce and cumin to the skillet containing remaining onions and garlic. Bring to a boil over medium-high heat, stirring occasionally.

5. Remove meatballs from the baking pan with a slotted spoon, and add meatballs to sauce. Bring to a boil, and simmer the meatballs, covered, over low heat, turning occasionally with a slotted spoon, for 15 minutes. Garnish with fresh thyme.

Note: The meatball mixture can be prepared up to 1 day in advance and refrigerated, tightly covered. Also, the dish can be cooked up to 2 days in advance and refrigerated, tightly covered. Reheat in a 350°F oven, covered, for 15 to 20 minutes, or until hot.

Variation:

✳ Use ground lamb instead of beef.

Meatballs are called *köfte* throughout the Islamic world, and Turkish cuisine alone includes more than eighty varieties.

Grilled Middle Eastern Beef Meatballs

Grilling ground meat on skewers is ubiquitous in Middle Eastern cooking. Because these kebabs contain no egg, they can be seared on the outside and enjoyed rare on the inside.

Makes 4 to 6 servings | Active time: 15 minutes | Start to finish: 30 minutes

8 to 12 (8-inch) bamboo skewers

1¼ pounds ground chuck

4 garlic cloves, minced

¼ cup grated red onion

¼ cup chopped fresh parsley

1 tablespoon ground coriander

2 teaspoons ground cumin

½ teaspoon ground cinnamon

Salt and freshly ground black pepper to taste

FOR DIPPING:

1 cup Middle Eastern Yogurt Sauce (page 33) or purchased hummus

1. Soak the bamboo skewers in cold water to cover. Prepare a medium-hot charcoal or gas grill, or preheat the oven broiler.

2. Combine beef, garlic, onion, parsley, coriander, cumin, cinnamon, salt, and pepper in a mixing bowl, and mix well.

3. Divide mixture into 8 to 12 portions, and form each portion into a sausage shape. Insert a skewer into each sausage so that the tip of the skewer is almost at the top of the meat.

4. Grill skewers for a total of 6 minutes, uncovered if using a charcoal grill, turning them gently with tongs to cook all sides. Serve immediately, accompanied by a bowl of Middle Eastern Yogurt Sauce for dipping.

Note: The beef mixture can be prepared up to 1 day in advance and refrigerated, tightly covered. Also, the skewers can be grilled up to 2 days in advance and refrigerated, tightly covered. Reheat them in a 350°F oven, covered, for 10 to 12 minutes, or until hot.

Variations:
* Make the meatballs from ground lamb or a combination of ground lamb and ground beef.
* Make the meatballs from ground turkey.

To add additional flavor to grilled skewered dishes, use large rosemary branches as skewers. Soak them in water as you would bamboo skewers. Once heated, they add aroma to the fire and the food.

Japanese Scallion Beef Meatballs

Negimaki—thin slices of beef rolled around scallions and then grilled—are a Japanese classic. These meatballs include all the same flavors and are perfect as hors d'oeuvre.

Makes 4 to 6 servings | *Active time: 15 minutes* | *Start to finish: 30 minutes*

1¼ pounds ground chuck

1 cup cooked white rice

1 bunch scallions, white parts and 3 inches of green tops, chopped

3 garlic cloves, minced

¼ cup soy sauce

2 tablespoons Asian sesame oil

1 tablespoon grated fresh ginger

¼ teaspoons Chinese five-spice powder

Freshly ground black pepper to taste

Vegetable oil spray

FOR DIPPING:

1 cup Sesame Honey Mustard Sauce (page 35)

1. Preheat the oven to 450°F. Line a rimmed baking sheet with heavy-duty aluminum foil, and spray the foil with vegetable oil spray.

2. Combine beef, rice, scallions, garlic, soy sauce, sesame oil, ginger, five-spice powder, and pepper in a mixing bowl, and mix well. Make mixture into 1½-inch meatballs, and arrange meatballs on the prepared pan. Spray tops of meatballs with vegetable oil spray.

3. Bake meatballs for 12 to 15 minutes, or until cooked through. Remove the pan from the oven, and serve immediately accompanied by a bowl of Sesame Honey Mustard Sauce for dipping.

Note: The beef mixture can be prepared up to 1 day in advance and refrigerated, tightly covered. Also, the meatballs can be baked up to 2 days in advance and refrigerated, tightly covered. Reheat them in a 350°F oven, covered, for 10 to 12 minutes, or until hot.

Variation:

∗ Make the meatballs from ground pork, and serve with Asian Dipping Sauce (page 25) rather than the more assertive mustard-based sauce.

Chinese Beef Meatballs with Peppers and Onions

This hearty dish is a variation on pepper steak, traditionally popular in Chinese-American restaurants. The rice is included in the meatballs, so the dinner is complete.

Makes 4 to 6 servings | Active time: 25 minutes | Start to finish: 50 minutes

1¼ pounds ground chuck

1 cup cooked white rice

4 scallions, white parts and 3 inches of green tops, chopped

4 garlic cloves, minced and divided

¼ cup soy sauce, divided

2 tablespoons dry sherry

2 tablespoons Asian sesame oil

Freshly ground black pepper to taste

1½ cups beef stock

3 tablespoons Chinese fermented black beans, finely chopped

2 tablespoons cornstarch

2 teaspoons granulated sugar

3 tablespoons vegetable oil

2 tablespoons grated fresh ginger

½ teaspoons red pepper flakes or to taste

1 large red onion, halved lengthwise and thinly sliced

2 bell peppers of any color, seeds and ribs removed, and thinly sliced

3 tablespoons chopped fresh cilantro

Vegetable oil spray

1. Preheat the oven to 450°F. Line a rimmed baking sheet with heavy-duty aluminum foil, and spray the foil with vegetable oil spray.

2. Combine beef, rice, scallions, 2 garlic cloves, 2 tablespoons soy sauce, sherry, sesame oil, and pepper in a mixing bowl, and mix well. Make mixture into 1½-inch meatballs, and arrange meatballs on the prepared pan. Spray tops of meatballs with vegetable oil spray. Combine stock, black beans, remaining soy sauce, cornstarch, and sugar in a bowl, and stir well to dissolve sugar. Set aside.

3. Bake meatballs for 12 to 15 minutes, or until cooked through. Remove the pan from the oven, and set aside. While meatballs bake, heat oil in a large skillet over high heat, swirling to coat. Add remaining 2 garlic cloves, ginger, and red pepper flakes, and stir-fry for 15 seconds, or until fragrant. Add onion and bell peppers and stir-fry for 2 minutes. Add sauce, and stir-fry for 2 minutes or until slightly thickened.

4. Remove meatballs from the baking pan with a slotted spoon, and add meatballs to the skillet. Cook 1 minute, and serve immediately, sprinkled with cilantro.

Note: The meatball mixture can be prepared up to 1 day in advance and refrigerated, tightly covered. Also, the dish can be cooked up to 2 days in advance and refrigerated, tightly covered. Reheat in a 350°F oven, covered, for 15 to 20 minutes, or until hot.

Variation:

* Substitute pork or chicken in place of the beef, and use chicken stock instead of beef stock.

Chapter 4

Porcine Pleasures:

Meatballs with Pork, Sausage, and Ham

I'm constantly amazed at the versatility of pork. Because of pork's naturally subtle, delicate flavor, and buttery texture, it is somewhat similar to chicken. Pork can be flavored so many ways to achieve a variety of truly delicious results.

Perhaps it's these qualities that has made pork the meat of choice to sausage-makers around the world who flavor the pork with everything from herbs and chiles to nuts and fruits. And remember, pork can also be smoked and/or cured to become ham, enjoyed as much in Parma as in Pasadena.

During the past few decades American pork has been bred to be lower in fat, thus the ad campaign about "the other white meat." Another advantage to cooking with pork is that it is relatively inexpensive; even the prized tenderloins sell for a fraction of the price of beef tenderloins or racks of lamb.

The recipes in this chapter are quick and casual because much of the seasoning is in the sausage itself. But you'll find dishes that are also elegant enough for entertaining.

Crunchy Pork Meatballs in Bourbon Barbecue Sauce

Water chestnuts were one of the first Asian ingredients adopted by American cooks because they give food a crunchy texture; even fifty years ago they were being included in non-Asian dishes. This recipe is an updated version of the classic meatballs in barbecue sauce; it's laced with bourbon and mustard.

Makes 4 to 6 servings | *Active time: 20 minutes* | *Start to finish: 45 minutes*

2 tablespoons vegetable oil

1 large onion, chopped

4 garlic cloves, minced

1 large egg

2 tablespoons whole milk

3 pieces whole wheat bread

1 (8-ounce) can water chestnuts, drained, rinsed, and chopped

2 tablespoons chopped fresh parsley

2 tablespoons chopped fresh sage or 1 tablespoon dried

1¼ pounds ground pork

Salt and freshly ground black pepper to taste

1 cup Southern Barbecue Sauce (page 23) or purchased barbecue sauce

¾ cup chicken stock

½ cup bourbon

¼ cup firmly packed light brown sugar

2 tablespoons grainy Dijon mustard

2 teaspoons cornstarch

Vegetable oil spray

1. Preheat the oven broiler. Line a rimmed baking sheet with heavy-duty aluminum foil, and spray the foil with vegetable oil spray.

2. Heat oil in a large skillet over medium-high heat. Add onion and garlic and cook, stirring frequently, for 3 minutes, or until onion is translucent. While vegetables cook, combine egg and milk in a mixing bowl, and whisk until smooth. Break bread into tiny pieces and add to mixing bowl along with water chestnuts, parsley, and sage, and mix well.

3. Add ½ of onion mixture and pork, season to taste with salt and pepper, and mix well again. Make mixture into 1½-inch meatballs, and arrange meatballs on the prepared pan. Spray tops of meatballs with vegetable oil spray.

4. Broil meatballs 6 inches from the broiler element, turning them with tongs to brown all sides. While meatballs brown, add barbecue sauce, stock, bourbon, brown sugar, and mustard to the skillet. Bring to a boil over medium-high heat, stirring occasionally. Simmer sauce over low heat, uncovered, for 10 minutes.

5. Remove meatballs from the baking pan with a slotted spoon, and add meatballs to sauce. Bring to a boil, and simmer the meatballs, covered, over low heat, turning occasionally with a slotted spoon, for 15 minutes. Mix cornstarch with 1 tablespoon cold water in a small bowl, and add to sauce. Cook for 1 minute, or until slightly thickened. Season to taste with salt and pepper, and serve immediately.

Note: The pork mixture can be prepared up to 1 day in advance and refrigerated, tightly covered. Also, the dish can be cooked up to 2 days in advance and refrigerated, tightly covered. Reheat it in a 350°F oven, covered, for 15 to 20 minutes, or until hot.

Variation:
✻ Use ground turkey in place of ground pork.

Crunchy Southwestern Pork Meatballs

The assertive flavors of traditional Southwestern cooking remain popular in the pantheon of American regional cuisines, and this easy recipe includes many of them. The crushed tortilla chips add texture to the meatballs, too.

Makes 4 to 6 servings | Active time: 20 minutes | Start to finish: 35 minutes

2 slices white bread

2 tablespoons whole milk

2 tablespoons olive oil

½ small red onion, finely chopped

2 garlic cloves, minced

1 tablespoon chili powder

1 teaspoon ground cumin

½ teaspoon dried oregano

1 large egg

½ cup tortilla chips (crushed in heavy-duty plastic bag)

3 tablespoons chopped fresh cilantro

1¼ pounds ground pork

Salt and freshly ground black pepper to taste

Vegetable oil spray

FOR DIPPING:

1 cup Mexican Tomato Sauce (page 21) or bottled salsa, heated

1. Preheat the oven to 450°F. Line a rimmed baking sheet with heavy-duty aluminum foil, and spray the foil with vegetable oil spray. Tear bread into small pieces, and place bread in a bowl with milk; stir well.

2. Heat oil in a small skillet over medium-high heat. Add onion and garlic, and cook, stirring frequently, for 3 minutes, or until onion is translucent. Add chili powder, cumin, and oregano, and cook, stirring constantly, for 1 minute. While vegetables cook, whisk egg in a mixing bowl, and add bread mixture, crushed tortilla chips, and cilantro, and mix well.

3. Add onion mixture and pork to the mixing bowl, season to taste with salt and pepper, and mix well again. Make mixture into 1½-inch meatballs, and arrange meatballs on the prepared pan. Spray tops of meatballs with vegetable oil spray.

4. Bake meatballs for 12 to 15 minutes, or until cooked through. Remove the pan from the oven, and serve immediately, accompanied by a bowl of Mexican Tomato Sauce for dipping.

Note: The pork mixture can be prepared up to 1 day in advance and refrigerated, tightly covered. Also, the meatballs can be baked up to 2 days in advance and refrigerated, tightly covered. Reheat them in a 350°F oven, covered, for 10 to 12 minutes, or until hot.

Variation:
✳ Make the meatballs from ground chicken or turkey.

Heat and light are enemies of dried herbs and spices. Keep herbs in a cool, dark place to preserve their potency.

Sausage Meatballs with Plums and Wine Sauce

Cooking sausages with fruit is common in German and other Northern European cuisines, and using flavorful and spicy Italian sausage balances the sweetness of the fruit. Serve these with plenty of the flavorful sauce.

Makes 4 to 6 servings | *Active time: 20 minutes* | *Start to finish: 1 hour*

¾ cup granulated sugar

¾ cup red wine vinegar

½ cup dry red wine

1 (3-inch) cinnamon stick

4 whole cloves

6 ripe purple plums

1 large egg

2 tablespoons chicken stock or water

½ cup plain breadcrumbs

2 tablespoons chopped fresh parsley

1¼ pounds bulk sweet Italian sausage

Salt and freshly ground black pepper to taste

2 teaspoons cornstarch

Vegetable oil spray

1. Combine sugar, vinegar, wine, cinnamon stick, and cloves in a non-reactive saucepan, and bring to a boil over medium-high heat, stirring occasionally. Simmer 5 minutes, then add plums, cover the pan, and simmer plums for 10 minutes over low heat. Remove plums from the pan with a slotted spoon, reserving poaching liquid. When cool enough to handle, remove and discard stones and slice fruit. Set aside.

2. While plums poach, preheat the oven broiler. Line a rimmed baking sheet with heavy-duty aluminum foil, and spray the foil with vegetable oil spray.

3. Combine egg, stock, breadcrumbs, and parsley in a mixing bowl, and mix well. Add sausage, season to taste with salt and pepper, and mix well again. Make mixture into 1½-inch meatballs, and arrange meatballs on the prepared pan. Spray tops of meatballs with vegetable oil spray.

4. Broil meatballs 6-inches from the broiler element, turning them with tongs to brown all sides.

5. Remove meatballs from the baking pan with a slotted spoon, and add meatballs to reserved poaching liquid. Bring to a boil, and simmer meatballs, covered, over low heat, turning occasionally with a slotted spoon, for 15 minutes. Remove meatballs from the pan with a slotted spoon, and add to plum slices.

6. Cook poaching liquid over medium-high heat until reduced by ½. Mix cornstarch with 1 tablespoon cold water in a small bowl, and add to sauce. Cook for 1 minute, or until slightly thickened. Return meatballs and plums to sauce to reheat, and serve immediately.

Note: The pork mixture can be prepared up to 1 day in advance and refrigerated, tightly covered. Also, the dish can be cooked up to 2 days in advance and refrigerated, tightly covered. Reheat it in a 350°F oven, covered, for 15 to 20 minutes, or until hot.

Variations:
* If you find fresh kielbasa sausage, it's great in this recipe.
* Use bulk maple-flavored pork sausage.

Ham Meatballs with Italian Vegetable Sauce

The saltiness of ham complements the robust tomato and vegetable sauce in which these meatballs are finished. Serve them on pasta accompanied by a green salad.

Makes 4 to 6 servings | *Active time: 20 minutes* | *Start to finish: 40 minutes*

¼ cup olive oil

3 medium onions, halved and thinly sliced

1 green bell pepper, seeds and ribs removed, and thinly sliced

1 red bell pepper, seeds and ribs removed, and thinly sliced

3 garlic cloves, minced

1 (14.5-ounce) can crushed tomatoes, undrained

1 (8-ounce) can tomato sauce

½ cup dry white wine, divided

2 tablespoons chopped fresh parsley

1 tablespoon Italian seasoning

1 bay leaf

1 large egg

½ cup seasoned Italian breadcrumbs

1 pound cooked ham, finely chopped

½ pound ground pork

Salt and freshly ground black pepper to taste

Vegetable oil spray

1. Heat oil in a large skillet over medium-high heat. Add onions, green pepper, red pepper, and garlic, and cook, stirring frequently, for 3 minutes, or until onions are translucent. Add tomatoes, tomato sauce, ¼ cup wine, parsley, Italian seasoning, and bay leaf. Bring to a boil over medium-high heat, stirring occasionally. Reduce the heat to low and simmer sauce, uncovered, for 15 minutes.

2. While sauce simmers, preheat the oven broiler. Line a rimmed baking sheet with heavy-duty aluminum foil, and spray the foil with vegetable oil spray.

3. Combine egg, remaining ¼ cup wine, and breadcrumbs in a mixing bowl, and whisk until smooth. Add ham and pork, season to taste with salt and pepper, and mix well again. Make mixture into 1½-inch meatballs, and arrange meatballs on the prepared pan. Spray tops of meatballs with vegetable oil spray.

4. Broil meatballs 6 inches from the broiler element, turning them with tongs to brown all sides. Remove meatballs from the baking pan with a slotted spoon, and add meatballs to sauce. Bring to a boil, and simmer meatballs, covered, over low heat, turning occasionally with a slotted spoon, for 15 minutes. Remove and discard bay leaf, season to taste with salt and pepper, and serve immediately.

Note: The pork mixture can be prepared up to 1 day in advance and refrigerated, tightly covered. Also, the dish can be cooked up to 2 days in advance and refrigerated, tightly covered. Reheat it in a 350°F oven, covered, for 15 to 20 minutes, or until hot.

Variations:

✳ Use Italian sausage rather than chopped ham and pork for the meatballs and it will be spicier.

✳ Use ground turkey and poultry ham if you want to avoid red meats.

Italian Lemon and Rosemary Pork Meatballs

When traveling in Umbria I fell in love with porchetta, slowly roasted pork shoulder or loin stuffed with rosemary and garlic and drizzled with lemon. All those flavors appear in this quick and easy meatball version.

Makes 4 to 6 servings | Active time: 20 minutes | Start to finish: 35 minutes

3 slices white bread

¼ cup whole milk

2 tablespoons olive oil

2 shallots, chopped

6 garlic cloves, minced

1 large egg

Zest and juice of 2 lemons

¼ cup freshly grated Parmesan

3 tablespoons chopped fresh rosemary or 1 tablespoon dried

2 tablespoons chopped fresh parsley

1¼ pounds ground pork

Salt and freshly ground black pepper to taste

Vegetable oil spray

1. Preheat the oven to 450°F. Line a rimmed baking sheet with heavy-duty aluminum foil, and spray the foil with vegetable oil spray. Tear bread into small pieces, and place bread in a bowl with milk; stir well.

2. Heat oil in a small skillet over medium-high heat. Add shallots and garlic, and cook, stirring frequently, for 3 minutes, or until translucent.

While vegetables cook, whisk egg in a mixing bowl, and add bread mixture, lemon zest, Parmesan, rosemary, and parsley, and mix well.

3. Add shallot mixture and pork to the mixing bowl, season to taste with salt and pepper, and mix well again. Make mixture into 1½-inch meatballs, and arrange meatballs on the prepared pan. Spray tops of meatballs with vegetable oil spray.

4. Bake meatballs for 12 to 15 minutes, or until cooked through. Remove the pan from the oven, drizzle lemon juice over meatballs, and serve immediately.

Note: The pork mixture can be prepared up to 1 day in advance and refrigerated, tightly covered. Also, the meatballs can be baked up to 2 days in advance and refrigerated, tightly covered. Reheat them in a 350°F oven, covered, for 10 to 12 minutes, or until hot.

Variation:

＊ Make the meatballs from ground veal or ground chicken.

Zest really does have something to do with zesty; it's the thin, colored outer portion of citrus skin that contains all the aromatic oils. The white pith just beneath it is bitter, so take pains to separate the zest from the fruit without also taking any pith with it. Remove the zest using a special citrus zester, a vegetable peeler, or a paring knife. You can also grate it using the fine holes of a box grater.

Mexican Pork and Zucchini Meatballs

Zucchini adds both subtle flavor and texture to this zesty Mexican dish. Serve it with some saffron rice, and top it with guacamole and salsa, if you wish.

Makes 4 to 6 servings | *Active time: 20 minutes* | *Start to finish: 45 minutes*

3 tablespoons olive oil

1 medium onion, chopped

1 small zucchini, finely chopped

3 garlic cloves, minced

1 large egg

2 tablespoons whole milk

½ cup plain breadcrumbs

1 tablespoon dried oregano

1 teaspoon ground cumin

1¼ pounds ground pork

Salt and freshly ground black pepper to taste

1 (28-ounce) can crushed tomatoes in tomato puree

1 or 2 chipotle chiles in adobo sauce, drained

¼ cup chopped fresh cilantro

Vegetable oil spray

1. Preheat the oven broiler. Line a rimmed baking sheet with heavy-duty aluminum foil, and spray the foil with vegetable oil spray.

2. Heat oil in a skillet over medium-high heat. Add onion, zucchini, and garlic, and cook, stirring frequently, for 3 minutes, or until onion is translucent. While vegetables cook, combine egg and milk in a mixing bowl, and whisk until smooth. Add breadcrumbs, oregano, and cumin, and mix well.

3. Add onion mixture and pork, season to taste with salt and pepper, and mix well again. Make mixture into 2-inch meatballs, and arrange meatballs on the prepared pan. Spray tops of meatballs with vegetable oil spray.

4. Broil meatballs 6 inches from the broiler element, turning them with tongs to brown all sides. While meatballs brown, combine tomatoes and chiles in a blender or food processor, and puree until smooth. Pour mixture into a saucepan, and stir in cilantro. Bring to a boil over medium-high heat, stirring occasionally.

5. Remove meatballs from the baking pan with a slotted spoon, and add meatballs to sauce. Bring to a boil, and simmer meatballs, covered, over low heat, turning occasionally with a slotted spoon, for 15 minutes. Serve immediately.

Note: The pork mixture can be prepared up to 1 day in advance and refrigerated, tightly covered. Also, the dish can be cooked up to 2 days in advance and refrigerated, tightly covered. Reheat it in a 350°F oven, covered, for 15 to 20 minutes, or until hot.

Variation:
* Make the meatballs from ground chicken or turkey.

Zucchini is Italian in origin, and its native name was retained when it was integrated into American cooking. Choose small zucchini because they tend to have a sweeter flavor and the seeds are tender and less pronounced.

Steamed Chinese Pork Meatballs

Rice-coated steamed meatballs are one of my favorite dim sum treats. I never realized how easy they are to make at home until I began developing this recipe. Serve with some fried rice or lo mein and some stir-fried vegetables.

Makes 4 to 6 servings | Active time: 20 minutes | Start to finish: 5 hours, including 4 hours to soak rice

2 cups glutinous (sticky) rice

½ cup dried shiitake mushrooms

1 large egg

2 tablespoons soy sauce

1½ tablespoons cornstarch

2 teaspoons granulated sugar

½ cup finely chopped water chestnuts

½ cup panko breadcrumbs

3 tablespoons chopped fresh cilantro

2 garlic cloves, minced

2 scallions, white parts and 2-inches of green tops, rinsed, trimmed, and chopped

1 tablespoon grated fresh ginger

1 teaspoon granulated sugar

1¼ pounds ground pork

Vegetable oil spray

FOR DIPPING:

1 cup Sweet and Sour Sauce (page 25) or purchased sauce, heated

1. Soak rice covered with cold water in a mixing bowl for 4 hours, or preferably overnight. Once soaked, drain rice well, and place it on a lint-free cloth.

2. Combine shiitake mushrooms and 1 cup boiling water in a bowl, pushing them down into the water. Soak for 10 minutes, then drain mushrooms and reserve soaking liquid. Discard stems, and chop mushrooms. Set aside.

3. Combine egg, 2 tablespoons mushroom soaking liquid, soy sauce, cornstarch, and sugar in a mixing bowl, and whisk until smooth. Add mushrooms, water chestnuts, breadcrumbs, cilantro, garlic, scallions, ginger, sugar, and pork, and mix well.

4. Make mixture into 1½-inch balls, and roll balls in rice, pressing it in. Spray bamboo steamer baskets with vegetable oil spray, and arrange meatballs in baskets.

5. Steam meatballs for 30 to 35 minutes, and serve immediately, accompanied by a bowl Sweet and Sour Sauce for dipping.

Note: The pork mixture can be prepared up to 1 day in advance and refrigerated, tightly covered. Also, the meatballs can be steamed up to 2 days in advance and refrigerated, tightly covered. Reheat them in the steamer for 5 to 10 minutes, or until hot.

Variation:

* Ground turkey or ground veal are equally good as the basis for the meatballs.

Although fresh shiitake mushrooms are relative newcomers to the American produce section, they are the granddaddy of all cultivated mushrooms. The Japanese have been cultivating them for more than 2,000 years. The ancient Greeks and Romans did not cultivate mushrooms; they merely encouraged wild ones to grow. It was not until the eighteenth century, when Olivier de Serres was agronomist to French King Louis XIV, that mushroom cultivation began in Europe.

Beijing Pork Meatballs

I made this recipe up one day to entice a friend's young child into eating more vegetables. It was so delicious it became part of my repertoire.

Makes 4 to 6 servings | *Active time: 20 minutes* | *Start to finish: 35 minutes*

2 tablespoons Asian sesame oil

1 tablespoon vegetable oil

3 scallions, white parts and 2-inches of green tops, chopped

3 garlic cloves, minced

1 tablespoon grated fresh ginger

1 tablespoon fermented black beans, chopped

1 carrot, finely chopped

1 celery rib, finely chopped

1 large egg

3 tablespoon hoisin sauce

1 tablespoon soy sauce

1 tablespoon Chinese chili paste with garlic

½ cup cooked white rice

1¼ pounds ground pork

¼ cup sesame seeds

Vegetable oil spray

FOR DIPPING:

1 cup Sesame Honey Mustard Sauce (page 35)

1. Preheat the oven to 450°F. Line a rimmed baking sheet with heavy-duty aluminum foil, and spray the foil with vegetable oil spray.

2. Heat sesame oil and vegetable oil in a skillet over medium-high heat. Add scallions, garlic, ginger, and black beans, and cook, stirring frequently, for 1 minute. Add carrot and celery, and cook, stirring frequently, for 3 minutes. While vegetables cook, whisk egg, hoisin sauce, soy sauce, and chili paste in a mixing bowl. Add rice, and mix well.

3. Add vegetable mixture and pork to the mixing bowl, and mix well again. Make mixture into 1½-inch meatballs, and arrange meatballs on the prepared pan. Spray tops of meatballs with vegetable oil spray.

4. Bake meatballs for 12 to 15 minutes, or until cooked through. Remove the pan from the oven, sprinkle with sesame seeds, and serve immediately accompanied by a bowl of Sesame Honey Mustard Sauce for dipping.

Note: The pork mixture can be prepared up to 1 day in advance and refrigerated, tightly covered. Also, the meatballs can be baked up to 2 days in advance and refrigerated, tightly covered. Reheat them in a 350°F oven, covered, for 10 to 12 minutes, or until hot.

Variation:

✳ Substitute ground chicken or ground turkey for the pork.

> Fermented black beans are tiny black soybeans preserved in salt, so they have a very pungent flavor. They should be chopped to release their flavor prior to cooking. Because they are preserved with salt, they last up to 2 years if refrigerated once opened.

Sausage, Cheddar, and Red Pepper Meatballs

The combination of cheddar and sausage is quintessentially American, and I like the addition of lots of sweet red bell peppers. These are always a hit when served as a hors d'oeuvre or at brunch along with scrambled eggs.

Makes 4 to 6 servings | Active time: 20 minutes | Start to finish: 35 minutes

2 tablespoons olive oil

1 large red bell pepper, seeds and ribs removed, and chopped

3 scallions, white parts only, chopped

2 garlic cloves, minced

1 large egg

2 tablespoons whole milk

1 cup seasoned Italian breadcrumbs, divided

¾ cup grated cheddar cheese

3 tablespoons chopped fresh parsley

2 teaspoons fresh thyme
or ½ teaspoon dried

1¼ pounds bulk breakfast sausage

Salt and freshly ground black pepper to taste

Vegetable oil spray

FOR DIPPING:

1 cup Herbed Tomato Sauce (page 21) or purchased marinara sauce, heated

1. Preheat the oven to 450°F. Line a rimmed baking sheet with heavy-duty aluminum foil, and spray the foil with vegetable oil spray.

2. Heat oil in a skillet over medium-high heat. Add red peppers, scallions, and garlic, and cook, stirring frequently, for 5 minutes, or until peppers are soft. While vegetables cook, whisk egg and milk in a mixing bowl, add ½ cup breadcrumbs, cheddar, parsley, and thyme, and mix well.

3. Add vegetable mixture and sausage to the mixing bowl, season to taste with salt and pepper, and mix well again. Make mixture into 1½-inch meatballs, and roll meatballs in remaining breadcrumbs. Arrange meatballs on the prepared pan, and spray tops of meatballs with vegetable oil spray.

4. Bake meatballs for 12 to 15 minutes, or until cooked through. Remove the pan from the oven, and serve immediately accompanied by a bowl of Herbed Tomato Sauce for dipping.

Note: The sausage mixture can be prepared up to 1 day in advance and refrigerated, tightly covered. Also, the meatballs can be baked up to 2 days in advance and refrigerated, tightly covered. Reheat them in a 350°F oven, covered, for 10 to 12 minutes, or until hot.

Variation:
* Substitute ground pork, veal, or turkey for the sausage if you want a dish with milder flavor.

> Bell peppers are hard to deal with because they don't sit flat on the cutting board. It's easier to slice and dice bell peppers from the inside out. Once the seeds and ribs have been removed, place the shiny, slippery skin on a cutting board; it's easier to control your knife and cut the size pieces you desire.

English Pork Meatballs

In traditional English cooking these meatballs are called "faggots," and they are traditionally served with mashed potatoes and peas. While authentic recipes call for using pork innards, I've adapted the recipe to use ground pork.

Makes 4 to 6 servings | Active time: 20 minutes | Start to finish: 1 hour

2 tablespoons vegetable oil

2 tablespoons unsalted butter

4 large onions, thinly sliced

Salt and freshly ground black pepper to taste

2 teaspoons granulated sugar

½ cup dry white wine

2 cups chicken stock

2 tablespoons chopped fresh parsley

2 teaspoons fresh thyme or ½ teaspoon dried

Salt and freshly ground black pepper to taste

1 large egg

2 tablespoons whole milk

½ cup plain breadcrumbs

¼ teaspoon ground nutmeg

1¼ pounds ground pork

2 teaspoons cornstarch

Vegetable oil spray

1. Heat oil and butter in a large skillet over medium heat. Add onions, and toss to coat. Cover the pan, and cook onions for 10 minutes, stirring occasionally. Sprinkle onions with salt, pepper, and sugar, and raise the heat to medium-high. Cook onions for 15 to 20 minutes, stirring occasionally, or until brown. Add wine, and cook over high heat for 1 minute, stirring constantly. Add stock, parsley, and thyme, and bring to a boil over medium-high heat. Reduce the heat to low, and simmer sauce, uncovered, for 5 minutes.

2. While onions cook, preheat the oven broiler. Line a rimmed baking sheet with heavy-duty aluminum foil, and spray the foil with vegetable oil spray. Combine egg and milk in a mixing bowl, and whisk until smooth. Add breadcrumbs and nutmeg to the mixing bowl, and mix well. Add pork, season to taste with salt and pepper, and mix well.

3. Make mixture into 2-inch meatballs, and arrange meatballs on the prepared pan. Spray tops of meatballs with vegetable oil spray. Broil meatballs 6 inches from the broiler element, turning them with tongs to brown all sides. Remove the pan from the oven, and set aside.

4. Add meatballs to sauce, bring to a boil, and simmer meatballs, covered, over low heat, turning occasionally with a slotted spoon, for 15 minutes.

Combine cornstarch and 1 tablespoon cold water in a small bowl, and stir well. Add mixture to sauce, and cook for an additional 2 minutes, or until slightly thickened. Season sauce to taste with salt and pepper, and serve immediately.

Note: The pork mixture can be prepared up to 1 day in advance and refrigerated, tightly covered. Also, the dish can be cooked up to 2 days in advance and refrigerated, tightly covered. Reheat it in a 350°F oven, covered, for 15 to 20 minutes, or until hot.

Variation:

* Substitute ground turkey for the pork.

There's no question; the most time-consuming part of this dish is caramelizing the onions. Make a double or triple batch and freeze what's not needed for this recipe to use in other dishes.

Chapter 5

Meating the Challenge:

Meatballs Made from Veal and Lamb

While ground beef, ground pork, and sausage have been fixtures in the meat case for generations, grinding lamb and delicate veal is a recent phenomenon. This is truly a shame, because the ground form is the most affordable for enjoying the flavor of these luxury meats.

Veal dishes tend to be Italian, such as Veal Meatballs Parmigiana and Veal Meatballs Marsala, or originate in Northern Europe, such as our Dilled Scandinavian Veal Meatballs.

The same is not true for lamb; it's a world traveler. It is popular in countries bordering the Mediterranean, as well as in the Middle East. It has long been the favorite meat in Greek cooking and plays an important role in Spain's culinary heart, too. Lamb is also very well represented in Persian and Indian dishes.

Veal Meatballs Parmigiana

Veal parmigiana is an Italian-American invention. You'd be hard pressed to find it on a menu in Italy. But we love it. This meatball version is easy to make and ideal to serve at a buffet dinner. All you need is a tossed salad and some crusty garlic bread.

Makes 4 to 6 servings | Active time: 25 minutes | Start to finish: 1 hour

3 tablespoons olive oil

1 medium onion, chopped

3 garlic cloves, minced

1 large egg

2 tablespoons whole milk

3 pieces white sandwich bread

2 tablespoons chopped fresh parsley

1¼ pounds ground veal

Salt and freshly ground black pepper to taste

2 cups Herbed Tomato Sauce (page 21) or purchased marinara sauce

2 cups grated whole milk mozzarella

¼ cup freshly grated Parmesan

Vegetable oil spray

1. Preheat the oven broiler. Line a rimmed baking sheet with heavy-duty aluminum foil, and spray the foil with vegetable oil spray.

2. Heat oil in a large skillet over medium-high heat. Add onion and garlic and cook, stirring frequently, for 3 minutes, or until onion is translucent. While vegetables cook, combine egg and milk in a mixing bowl, and whisk until smooth. Break bread into tiny pieces and add to mixing bowl along with parsley, and mix well.

3. Add onion mixture and veal, season to taste with salt and pepper, and mix well again. Make mixture into 1½-inch meatballs, and arrange meatballs on the prepared pan. Spray tops of meatballs with vegetable oil spray.

4. Broil meatballs 6 inches from the broiler element, turning them with tongs to brown all sides. While meatballs brown, heat Herbed Tomato Sauce in a large skillet over medium-high heat, stirring occasionally.

5. Remove meatballs from the baking pan with a slotted spoon, and add meatballs to sauce. Bring to a boil, and simmer meatballs, covered, over low heat, turning occasionally with a slotted spoon, for 15 minutes. Season to taste with salt and pepper, and reheat the oven broiler.

6. Transfer meatballs and sauce to a 9x13-inch baking pan, and sprinkle mozzarella and Parmesans over meatballs. Broil 6 inches from the broiler element for 2 minutes, or until cheese is bubbly and browned. Serve immediately.

Note: The veal mixture can be prepared up to 1 day in advance and refrigerated, tightly covered. Also, the dish can be cooked up to 2 days in advance and refrigerated, tightly covered. Reheat in a 350°F oven, covered, for 15 to 20 minutes, or until hot.

Variation:

∗ Substitute ground chicken or turkey for the veal.

> **Meatballs played a role in a famous ad campaign in the 1960s when the phrase "Mamma Mia! That's a some spicy meatball!" entered the vernacular as an ad for Alka Seltzer.**

Dilled Scandinavian Veal Meatballs

Veal is rarely used in Scandinavian cooking, with these lightly seasoned meatballs being an exception. The light dill cream sauce is luscious. Serve this with buttered egg noodles.

Makes 4 to 6 servings | Active time: 25 minutes | Start to finish: 50 minutes

4 tablespoons (½ stick) unsalted butter, divided

1 small onion, chopped

1 large egg

2 tablespoons whole milk

3 slices white sandwich bread

Pinch ground nutmeg

Pinch ground allspice

Pinch ground ginger

1¼ pounds ground veal

Salt and freshly ground black pepper to taste

3 tablespoons all-purpose flour

1 cup chicken stock

⅔ cup light cream

¼ cup chopped fresh dill

¼ cup chopped fresh parsley or dill for garnish, if desired

Vegetable oil spray

1. Preheat the oven broiler. Line a rimmed baking sheet with heavy-duty aluminum foil, and spray the foil with vegetable oil spray.

2. Heat 2 tablespoons butter in a large skillet over medium-high heat. Add onion, and cook, stirring frequently, for 3 minutes, or until onion is translucent. While onion cooks, combine egg and milk in a mixing bowl, and whisk until smooth. Break bread into tiny pieces and add to mixing bowl along with nutmeg, allspice, and ginger, and mix well.

3. Add onion and veal, season to taste with salt and pepper, and mix well again. Make mixture into 1½-inch meatballs, and arrange meatballs on the prepared pan. Spray tops of meatballs with vegetable oil spray.

4. Broil meatballs 6 inches from the broiler element, turning them with tongs to brown all sides. While meatballs brown, add remaining butter to the skillet, and heat over low heat. Stir in flour, and cook for 2 minutes, stirring constantly. Whisk in stock, cream, and dill. Bring to a boil over medium-high heat, reduce the heat to medium, and simmer sauce, uncovered, for 10 minutes.

5. Remove meatballs from the baking pan with a slotted spoon, and add meatballs to sauce. Bring to a boil, and simmer meatballs, covered, over low heat, turning occasionally with a slotted spoon, for 15 minutes. Season to taste with salt and pepper, as well as parsley and dill and serve immediately.

Note: The veal mixture can be prepared up to 1 day in advance and refrigerated, tightly covered. Also, the dish can be cooked up to 2 days in advance and refrigerated, tightly covered. Reheat in a 350°F oven, covered, for 15 to 20 minutes, or until hot.

Variation:
∗ Substitute ground pork, chicken, or turkey for the veal.

Anyone who has ever dropped an egg on the floor knows what a mess it is to clean up. Instead of rushing to mop up the egg with a roll of paper towels, cover the mess with lots of salt and let it stand for 20 minutes. After that time, the egg should be solid enough to sweep into a dust pan.

Grilled Chinese Veal Meatballs

Veal is not used in Asian cuisines, but it's delicious when grilled with Asian flavors. Some stir-fried vegetables and rice can complete your meal.

Makes 4 to 6 servings | Active time: 20 minutes | Start to finish: 35 minutes

8 to 12 (8-inch) bamboo skewers

1 large egg

3 tablespoons soy sauce

2 tablespoons dry sherry

½ cup panko breadcrumbs

½ cup finely chopped water chestnuts

6 scallions, white parts and 2 inches of green tops, thinly sliced

2 tablespoons grated fresh ginger

¼ cup chopped fresh cilantro

4 garlic cloves, minced

1¼ pounds ground veal

Freshly ground black pepper to taste

Vegetable oil spray

FOR DIPPING:

1 cup Asian Dipping Sauce (page 25)

1. Soak the bamboo skewers in cold water to cover. Prepare a medium-hot charcoal or gas grill, or preheat the oven broiler.

2. Whisk egg, soy sauce, and sherry in a mixing bowl, and add breadcrumbs, water chestnuts, scallions, ginger, cilantro, and garlic, and mix well. Add veal to the mixing bowl, season to taste with pepper, and mix well again.

4. Divide mixture into 8 to 12 portions, and form each portion into a sausage shape. Insert a skewer into each sausage so that the tip of the skewer is almost at the top of the meat.

5. Grill skewers for a total of 6 to 8 minutes, covered, turning them gently with tongs to cook all sides. Serve immediately, accompanied by a bowl of Asian Dipping Sauce.

Note: The veal mixture can be prepared up to 1 day in advance and refrigerated, tightly covered. Also, the skewers can be grilled up to 2 days in advance and refrigerated, tightly covered. Reheat them in a 350°F oven, covered, for 10 to 12 minutes, or until hot.

Variation:

＊ Substitute ground pork, chicken, or turkey for the veal.

Many a cook has suffered a scraped knuckle while grating fresh ginger. If the ginger knob is large, peel only the amount you think you'll need and hold on to the remainder. If you're down to a small part, impale it on a fork and use that as a handle while grating.

Veal Meatballs Marsala

Veal, like chicken and pork, is mildly flavored, and takes to a wide variety of seasonings and sauces. The heady Marsala wine, mushrooms, and herbs create a delicious mélange for the meatballs. Serve this over small pasta such as orzo.

Makes 4 to 6 servings | *Active time: 25 minutes* | *Start to finish: 50 minutes*

3 tablespoons olive oil

1 medium onion, chopped

6 garlic cloves, minced

1 large egg

2 tablespoons whole milk

3 pieces white sandwich bread

⅓ cup chopped fresh parsley, divided

1¼ pounds ground veal

Salt and freshly ground black pepper to taste

3 tablespoons unsalted butter

½ pound mushrooms, wiped with a damp paper towel, stemmed, and diced

3 tablespoons all-purpose flour

1 tablespoon chopped fresh oregano or 1 teaspoon dried

2 teaspoons fresh thyme or ½ teaspoon dried

1 cup chicken stock

⅔ cup sweet Marsala wine

Vegetable oil spray

1. Preheat the oven broiler. Line a rimmed baking sheet with heavy-duty aluminum foil, and spray the foil with vegetable oil spray.

2. Heat oil in a large skillet over medium-high heat. Add onion and garlic and cook, stirring frequently, for 3 minutes, or until onion is translucent. While vegetables cook, combine egg and milk in a mixing bowl, and whisk until smooth. Break bread into tiny pieces and add to mixing bowl along with 2 tablespoons parsley, and mix well.

3. Add ¼ of onion mixture and veal, season to taste with salt and pepper, and mix well again. Make mixture into 1½-inch meatballs, and arrange meatballs on the prepared pan. Spray tops of meatballs with vegetable oil spray. Scrape remaining onion mixture into a dish, and reserve.

4. Broil meatballs 6 inches from the broiler element, turning them with tongs to brown all sides. While meatballs brown, add butter to the skillet and heat over medium-high heat. Add mushrooms and cook, stirring frequently, for 3 minutes, or until mushrooms are soft. Stir in flour, oregano, and thyme into the skillet, and cook over low heat for 1 minute, stirring constantly. Add reserved onion mixture, and whisk in stock and Marsala. Bring to a boil over medium-high heat, reduce the heat to medium, and simmer sauce, uncovered, for 10 minutes.

5. Remove meatballs from the baking pan with a slotted spoon, and add meatballs to sauce. Bring to a boil, and simmer meatballs, covered, over low heat, turning occasionally with a slotted spoon, for 15 minutes. Season to taste with salt and pepper, and serve immediately.

Note: The veal mixture can be prepared up to 1 day in advance and refrigerated, tightly covered. Also, the dish can be cooked up to 2 days in advance and refrigerated, tightly covered. Reheat in a 350°F oven, covered, for 15 to 20 minutes, or until hot.

Variation:
❋ Substitute ground chicken or turkey for the veal.

> **Marsala, a fortified wine similar to Madeira and sherry, is made in Sicily from a variety of grapes grown around the town of Marsala.**

Grilled Tandoori Lamb Meatballs

Indian dishes called *tandoori* mean that they are cooked over high heat in a traditional round tandoor, or oven. Many traditional Indian breads such as naan are also cooked in these ovens. But an outdoor grill does just as good a job, and these are some of the most flavorful morsels you will ever eat.

Makes 4 to 6 servings | *Active time: 15 minutes* | *Start to finish: 30 minutes*

8 to 12 (8-inch) bamboo skewers
½ cup plain yogurt
1 large egg
3 garlic cloves, minced
3 scallions, chopped
1 tablespoon grated fresh ginger
2 tablespoons paprika
2 teaspoons ground coriander
2 teaspoons ground cumin
1 teaspoon granulated sugar
1 teaspoon ground ginger
⅛ teaspoon ground cinnamon
½ cup plain breadcrumbs
1¼ pounds ground lamb
Salt and cayenne to taste

FOR DIPPING:

1 cup Cucumber Raita (page 33)

1. Soak the bamboo skewers in cold water to cover. Prepare a medium-hot charcoal or gas grill, or preheat the oven broiler.

2. Combine yogurt, egg, garlic, scallions, ginger, paprika, coriander, cumin, sugar, ginger, cinnamon, and breadcrumbs, and mix well. Add lamb to the mixing bowl, season to taste with salt and cayenne, and mix well again.

3. Divide mixture into 8 to 12 portions, and form each portion into a sausage shape. Insert a skewer into each sausage so that the tip of the skewer is almost at the top of the meat.

4. Grill skewers for a total of 6 to 8 minutes, uncovered if using a charcoal grill, turning them gently with tongs to cook all sides. Serve immediately, accompanied by a bowl of Cucumber Raita for dipping.

Note: The lamb mixture can be prepared up to 1 day in advance and refrigerated, tightly covered. Also, the skewers can be grilled up to 2 days in advance and refrigerated, tightly covered. Reheat them in a 350°F oven, covered, for 10 to 12 minutes, or until hot.

Variation:

✳ Substitute ground chuck, chicken, or turkey for the lamb.

Ground coriander is the seed of the same plant that produces cilantro as fresh leaves, although each flavor is entirely different. Coriander is one of the world's earliest recorded ingredients. Seeds were discovered in an Egyptian tomb that dates from 960 BCE.

Spanish Lamb Meatballs in Almond Sauce

Spanish and Middle Eastern cooking feature many of the same ingredients, stemming from the period of Moorish rule over Spain. One of those ingredients is almonds. Here they add some crunchiness to the sauce.

Makes 4 to 6 servings | *Active time: 20 minutes* | *Start to finish: 45 minutes*

¼ cup olive oil

1 large onion, chopped

3 garlic cloves, minced

1 large egg

⅔ cup dry red wine, divided

½ cup seasoned Italian breadcrumbs

2 tablespoons chopped fresh parsley

2 tablespoons smoked Spanish paprika

1¼ pounds ground lamb

Salt and freshly ground black pepper to taste

½ cup blanched slivered almonds

1 cup beef stock

Vegetable oil spray

1. Preheat the oven broiler. Line a rimmed baking sheet with heavy-duty aluminum foil, and spray the foil with vegetable oil spray.

2. Heat oil in a large skillet over medium-high heat. Add onion and garlic and cook, stirring frequently, for 3 minutes, or until onion is translucent. While vegetables cook, combine egg and 2 tablespoons wine, and whisk until smooth. Add breadcrumbs, parsley, and paprika, and mix well.

3. Add ½ of onion mixture and lamb, season to taste with salt and pepper, and mix well again. Make mixture into 1½-inch meatballs, and arrange meatballs on the prepared pan. Spray tops of meatballs with vegetable oil spray.

4. Broil meatballs 6 inches from the broiler element, turning them with tongs to brown all sides. While meatballs brown, combine remaining onions and garlic, almonds, remaining wine, and stock in a blender or food processor , and puree until smooth. Return mixture to the skillet, and bring to a boil over medium-high heat, stirring occasionally. Reduce the heat to low, and simmer sauce for 10 minutes.

5. Remove meatballs from the baking pan with a slotted spoon, and add meatballs to sauce. Bring to a boil, and simmer the meatballs, covered, over low heat, turning occasionally with a slotted spoon, for 15 minutes. Serve immediately.

Note: The lamb mixture can be prepared up to 1 day in advance and refrigerated, tightly covered. Also, the dish can be prepared up to 2 days in advance and refrigerated, tightly covered. Reheat them in a 350°F oven, covered, for 15 to 20 minutes, or until hot.

Variation:

＊ Substitute ground chuck for the lamb.

> Botanically speaking, almonds are not a nut, although we certainly treat them as such. They are really a fruit, related to the peach. The fruit is called a drupe, and there's a hard woody shell surrounding the seed, which is the almond.

South African Curried Lamb Meatballs

These meatballs are based on a meatloaf native to South Africa called *bobotie*. A combination of apple, curry, and almonds lends flavor to the dish. Serve them with braised red cabbage and mashed potatoes.

Makes 4 to 6 servings | *Active time: 20 minutes* | *Start to finish: 35 minutes*

3 tablespoons unsalted butter

1 medium onion, chopped

1 Granny Smith apple, peeled, cored, and chopped

¼ cup blanched almonds, finely chopped

1 large egg

2 tablespoons whole milk

½ cup plain breadcrumbs

½ cup chopped raisins

2 tablespoons chopped fresh parsley

1 tablespoon curry powder

1 teaspoon granulated sugar

1¼ pounds ground lamb

Salt and freshly ground black pepper to taste

Vegetable oil spray

FOR DIPPING:

1 cup Herbed Tomato Sauce (page 21) or purchased marinara sauce, heated

1. Preheat the oven to 450°F. Line a rimmed baking sheet with heavy-duty aluminum foil, and spray the foil with vegetable oil spray.

2. Heat butter in a small skillet over medium-high heat. Add onion, apple, and almonds, and cook, stirring frequently, for 3 minutes, or until onion is translucent. While vegetables cook, whisk egg and milk in a mixing bowl, and add breadcrumbs, raisins, parsley, curry powder, and sugar, and mix well.

3. Add vegetable mixture and lamb to the mixing bowl, season to taste with salt and pepper, and mix well again. Make mixture into 1½-inch meatballs, and arrange meatballs on the prepared pan. Spray tops of meatballs with vegetable oil spray.

4. Bake meatballs for 12 to 15 minutes, or until cooked through. Remove the pan from the oven, and serve immediately, accompanied by a bowl of Herbed Tomato Sauce for dipping.

Note: The lamb mixture can be prepared up to 1 day in advance and refrigerated, tightly covered. Also, the meatballs can be baked up to 2 days in advance and refrigerated, tightly covered. Reheat them in a 350°F oven, covered, for 10 to 12 minutes, or until hot.

Variation:

＊ Substitute ground chuck for the lamb.

While I'm all in favor of advance preparation when cooking, one task you can't do in advance is to grate or chop apples and let them stand, or they will discolor quickly. Prepare apples right before they are to be joined with other ingredients.

Grilled Lamb and Pistachio Meatballs

Cooking with nuts, including bright green pistachio nuts, is an integral part of Middle Eastern cooking. These tasty treats are then grilled for even more flavor.

Makes 4 to 6 servings | Active time: 20 minutes | Start to finish: 35 minutes

8 to 12 (8-inch) bamboo skewers

3 tablespoons olive oil

½ cup coarsely chopped pistachio nuts

2 shallots, chopped

3 garlic cloves, chopped

1 large egg

2 tablespoons dry red wine

½ cup seasoned Italian breadcrumbs

2 tablespoons chopped fresh parsley

1 tablespoon fresh thyme
or 1 teaspoon dried

1 tablespoon ground cumin

1 tablespoon ground coriander

2 teaspoons grated lemon zest

1¼ pounds ground lamb

Salt and freshly ground black pepper to taste

Vegetable oil spray

FOR DIPPING:

1 cup Tahini (page 27)
or purchased hummus

1. Soak the bamboo skewers in cold water to cover. Prepare a medium-hot charcoal or gas grill, or preheat the oven broiler.

2. Heat oil in a small skillet over medium-high heat. Add pistachio nuts, shallots, and garlic, and cook, stirring frequently, for 3 minutes, or until shallots are translucent. While mixture cooks, whisk egg and wine in a mixing bowl, and add breadcrumbs, parsley, thyme, cumin, coriander, and lemon zest, and mix well.

3. Add nut mixture and lamb to the mixing bowl, season to taste with salt and pepper, and mix well again.

4. Divide mixture into 8 to 12 portions, and form each portion into a sausage shape. Insert a skewer into each sausage so that the tip of the skewer is almost at the top of the meat.

5. Grill skewers for a total of 6 to 8 minutes, uncovered if using a charcoal grill, turning them gently with tongs to cook all sides. Serve immediately, accompanied by a bowl of Tahini for dipping.

Note: The lamb mixture can be prepared up to 1 day in advance and refrigerated, tightly covered. Also, the skewers can be grilled up to 2 days in advance and refrigerated, tightly covered. Reheat them in a 350°F oven, covered, for 10 to 12 minutes, or until hot.

Variation:
✳ Substitute ground chuck for the lamb.

Native to the Middle East, pistachios are one of the oldest flowering nut trees. Archeological discoveries in Turkey show that humans were munching on these healthy nuts as early as 7000 BCE. Legend has it that the Queen of Sheba decreed that pistachios were food for royals only.

Lamb Meatballs in Herbed Red Wine Sauce

Tender morsels of lamb braised in a red wine sauce is one of my favorite winter stews, so I decided to create a comforting dish made with meatballs. Serve these with orzo or pappardelle noodles.

Makes 4 to 6 servings | *Active time: 25 minutes* | *Start to finish: 55 minutes*

3 tablespoons unsalted butter

1 medium onion, chopped

1 small carrot, chopped

2 garlic cloves, minced

1 large egg

2 tablespoons whole milk

½ cup seasoned Italian breadcrumbs

3 tablespoons chopped fresh rosemary or 1 tablespoon dried

2 tablespoons chopped fresh parsley

1¼ pounds ground lamb

Salt and freshly ground black pepper to taste

3 tablespoons all-purpose flour

1¼ cups dry red wine

1 cup beef stock

2 tablespoons tomato paste

1 tablespoon herbes de Provence

Vegetable oil spray

1. Preheat the oven broiler. Line a rimmed baking sheet with heavy-duty aluminum foil, and spray the foil with vegetable oil spray.

2. Heat butter in a large skillet over medium-high heat. Add onion, carrot, and garlic and cook, stirring frequently, for 3 minutes, or until onion is translucent. While vegetables cook, combine egg and milk in a mixing bowl, and whisk until smooth. Add breadcrumbs, rosemary, and parsley, and mix well.

3. Add ½ onion mixture and lamb, season to taste with salt and pepper, and mix well again. Make mixture into 1½-inch meatballs, and arrange meatballs on the prepared pan. Spray tops of meatballs with vegetable oil spray.

4. Broil meatballs 6 inches from the broiler element, turning them with tongs to brown all sides. While meatballs brown, stir flour into the skillet, and cook over low heat for 2 minutes, stirring constantly. Whisk

in wine, stock, tomato paste, and herbes de Provence. Bring to a boil over medium-high heat, reduce the heat to medium, and simmer sauce, uncovered, for 10 minutes.

5. Remove meatballs from the baking pan with a slotted spoon, and add meatballs to sauce. Bring to a boil, and simmer meatballs, covered, over low heat, turning occasionally with a slotted spoon, for 15 minutes. Season to taste with salt and pepper, and serve immediately.

Note: The lamb mixture can be prepared up to 1 day in advance and refrigerated, tightly covered. Also, the dish can be cooked up to 2 days in advance and refrigerated, tightly covered. Reheat in a 350°F oven, covered, for 15 to 20 minutes, or until hot.

Variation:
* Substitute ground chuck for the lamb.

Lamb Meatballs in Curried Coconut Sauce

Creamy coconut milk, succulent dried fruit, and curry powder create a sauce that transforms these lamb meatballs into an exotic adventure. Serve them over rice pilaf, with a simple vegetable dish such as steamed cauliflower or sautéed green beans.

Makes 4 to 6 servings | *Active time: 25 minutes* | *Start to finish: 55 minutes*

2 tablespoons Asian sesame oil

8 scallions, white parts and 2-inches of green tops, chopped

6 garlic cloves, minced

2 tablespoon grated fresh ginger

1 large egg

2 tablespoons soy sauce

½ cup panko breadcrumbs

2 tablespoons chopped fresh cilantro

1¼ pounds ground lamb

Salt and freshly ground black pepper to taste

3 tablespoons curry powder

1 (14-ounce) can coconut milk

½ cup chicken stock

½ cup chopped dried apricots

3 tablespoons dried currants

1 tablespoon cornstarch

¼ cup chopped fresh parsley for garnish, if desired

Vegetable oil spray

1. Preheat the oven broiler. Line a rimmed baking sheet with heavy-duty aluminum foil, and spray the foil with vegetable oil spray.

2. Heat oil in a large skillet over medium-high heat. Add scallions, garlic, and ginger, and cook, stirring frequently, for 3 minutes, or until scallions are translucent. While vegetables cook, combine egg and soy sauce in a mixing bowl, and whisk until smooth. Add breadcrumbs, and cilantro, and mix well.

3. Add ½ of scallion mixture and lamb, season to taste with salt and pepper, and mix well again. Make mixture into 1½-inch meatballs, and arrange meatballs on the prepared pan. Spray tops of meatballs with vegetable oil spray.

4. Broil meatballs 6 inches from the broiler element, turning them with tongs to brown all sides. While meatballs brown, add curry powder to the skillet and cook over low heat, stirring constantly, for 1 minute. Stir in coconut milk, stock, apricots, and currants. Bring to a boil over medium-high heat, reduce the heat to medium, and simmer sauce, uncovered, for 10 minutes.

5. Remove meatballs from the baking pan with a slotted spoon, and add meatballs to sauce. Bring to a boil, and simmer meatballs, covered, over low heat, turning occasionally with a slotted spoon, for 15 minutes. Combine cornstarch and 1 tablespoon cold water in a small bowl, and stir well. Add mixture to sauce, and cook for an additional 2 minutes, or until lightly thickened. Season to taste with salt, pepper, and parsley, and serve immediately.

Note: The lamb mixture can be prepared up to 1 day in advance and refrigerated, tightly covered. Also, the dish can be cooked up to 2 days in advance and refrigerated, tightly covered. Reheat in a 350°F oven, covered, for 15 to 20 minutes, or until hot.

Variations:

✱ Substitute ground chuck for the lamb.

✱ Substitute chopped prunes, raisins, or dried cranberries for the dried fruits listed.

Greek Lamb Meatballs

In Greek and Middle Eastern food, mint is used in savory dishes rather than in desserts. When used in moderation, as in this recipe, the flavor enlivens the other herbs but doesn't dominate them. Serve the meatballs accompanied by tabbouleh or a pasta salad.

Makes 4 to 6 servings | Active time: 20 minutes | Start to finish: 45 minutes

3 tablespoons olive oil

1 small onion, chopped

3 garlic cloves, minced

1 large egg

2 tablespoons whole milk

1 tablespoon freshly squeezed lemon juice

½ cup seasoned Italian breadcrumbs

3 tablespoons chopped fresh oregano or 2 teaspoons dried

2 tablespoons chopped fresh parsley

1 tablespoon chopped fresh mint

1¼ pounds ground lamb

Salt and freshly ground black pepper to taste

Vegetable oil spray

FOR DIPPING:

1 cup Middle Eastern Yogurt Sauce (page 33) or purchased hummus

1. Preheat the oven to 450°F. Line a rimmed baking sheet with heavy-duty aluminum foil, and spray the foil with vegetable oil spray.

2. Heat oil in a small skillet over medium-high heat. Add onion and garlic, and cook, stirring frequently, for 3 minutes, or until onion is translucent. While vegetables cook, whisk egg, milk, and lemon juice in a mixing bowl, and add breadcrumbs, oregano, parsley, and mint, and mix well.

3. Add vegetable mixture and lamb to the mixing bowl, season to taste with salt and pepper, and mix well again. Make mixture into 1½-inch meatballs, and arrange meatballs on the prepared pan. Spray tops of meatballs with vegetable oil spray.

4. Bake meatballs for 12 to 15 minutes, or until cooked through. Remove the pan from the oven, and serve immediately, accompanied by a bowl of Middle Eastern Yogurt Sauce for dipping.

Note: The lamb mixture can be prepared up to 1 day in advance and refrigerated, tightly covered. Also, the meatballs can be baked up to 2 days in advance and refrigerated, tightly covered. Reheat them in a 350°F oven, covered, for 10 to 12 minutes, or until hot.

Variation:
✳ Substitute ground chuck for the lamb.

> In Greek mythology mint was once a nymph named Mentha. Because she angered Persephone, Pluto's wife, she turned her into this aromatic herb as permanent revenge.

Chapter 6

Double Your Pleasure:
Meatballs with More Than One Meat

*I*n most chapters in this book, the centerpiece of the meatballs recipe is a single meat. It can be a red meat, a white meat, poultry, or even fish, but it's a singular flavor. But that's not the case with the following recipes. Here they are all made from a combination of meats, which adds a degree of complexity to the recipes and a depth of flavor to the resulting dishes.

Making meatballs from a combination of meats is nothing new; that's why as I've mentioned, in many supermarkets you'll find a pre-ground mixture of pork, beef, and veal called "meatloaf mix." In the case of these recipes, however, it should be called "meatball mix." Some of the great meatball recipes, like the Italian-American meatball and the traditional Swedish meatball, are made with a mix of meats.

Mixing beef and pork is a common combination; the beef adds richness while the pork is more subtle and lends its delicacy to the mixture. Most of these recipes are drawn from European cuisines, but you'll find some Latin American and American ones as well.

Traditional Italian-American Meatballs

After years of experimentation these are my favorite meatballs. The mixture of herbs and spices give it a complex flavor, and the cheeses add moisture.

Makes 4 to 6 servings | *Active time: 20 minutes* | *Start to finish: 50 minutes*

2 tablespoons olive oil

1 small onion, finely chopped

3 garlic cloves, minced

¼ teaspoon crushed red pepper flakes

1 large egg

2 tablespoons whole milk

½ cup seasoned Italian breadcrumbs

¼ cup freshly grated Parmesan

¼ cup grated whole-milk mozzarella

2 tablespoons chopped fresh parsley

1 teaspoon Italian seasoning

½ pound ground pork

½ pound ground chuck

¼ pound ground veal

Salt and freshly ground black pepper to taste

2 cups Herbed Tomato Sauce (page 21) or purchased marinara sauce

Vegetable oil spray

1. Preheat the oven broiler. Line a rimmed baking sheet with heavy-duty aluminum foil, and spray the foil with vegetable oil spray.

2. Heat oil in a large skillet over medium-high heat. Add onion, garlic, and red pepper flakes, and cook, stirring frequently, for 3 minutes, or until onion is translucent.

Combine egg and milk in a mixing bowl, and whisk until smooth. Add breadcrumbs, Parmesan, mozzarella cheese, parsley, and Italian seasoning, and mix well.

3. Add onion mixture, pork, beef, and veal, season to taste with salt and pepper, and mix well again. Make mixture into 1½-inch meatballs, and arrange meatballs on the prepared pan. Spray tops of meatballs with vegetable oil spray.

4. Broil meatballs 6 inches from the broiler element, turning them with tongs to brown all sides. While meatballs brown, heat Herbed Tomato Sauce in the skillet in which the vegetables cooked.

5. Remove meatballs from the baking pan with a slotted spoon, and add meatballs to sauce. Bring to a boil, and simmer meatballs, covered, over low heat, turning occasionally with a slotted spoon, for 15 minutes. Season to taste with salt and pepper, and serve immediately.

Note: The meatball mixture can be prepared up to 1 day in advance and refrigerated, tightly covered. Also, the dish can be cooked up to 2 days in advance and refrigerated, tightly covered. Reheat in a 350°F oven, covered, for 15 to 20 minutes, or until hot.

Variations:

✳ Use these meatballs in Easy Meatball Lasagna (page 119).

✳ For traditional spaghetti and meatballs, cook ½ to 1 pound pasta, and pass some freshly grated Parmesan on the side.

✳ Cut the cooked meatballs into small pieces and use as a pizza topping.

✳ For a meatball sandwich, make an indentation in the center of a roll or section of bread to accommodate the size of the meatballs. Then top the meatballs with grated or sliced mozzarella and bake the sandwich in a 375°F oven for 10 to 12 minutes, or until meatballs are hot and cheese melts.

Easy Meatball Lasagna

Once you have a cache of meatballs in the freezer, there's no end to how you can use them. This easy lasagna is one option, and it's made with par-boiled lasagna noodles so it's not necessary to cook the pasta first.

Makes 6 to 8 servings | Active time: 15 minutes | Start to finish: 1¼ hours

1 batch Traditional Italian-American Meatballs (page 117)

1½ cups water

1 (1-pound) box precooked lasagna noodles

1 (15-ounce) container part-skim ricotta

½ pound grated mozzarella

1 cup freshly grated Parmesan

1. Preheat the oven to 350°F. Grease a 9x13-inch baking pan.

2. Remove meatballs from sauce, cut in half, and set aside. Add water to sauce, and stir well. Spread 1 cup sauce in bottom of prepared pan. Arrange ⅓ noodles, slightly overlapping if necessary, atop sauce. Spread ½ of ricotta over noodles. Sprinkle with ½ of mozzarella cheese, ½ of meatballs and ¼ cup Parmesan. Top with 1 cup sauce. Repeat layering with noodles, ricotta, mozzarella, meatballs, and ¼ cup Parmesan. Arrange remaining noodles over. Spoon remaining sauce over, covering completely. Sprinkle with remaining ½ cup Parmesan. Cover pan tightly with aluminum foil, and place the pan on a baking sheet.

3. Bake for 1 hour, or until noodles are tender and dish is bubbly. Increase the oven temperature to 400°F, remove and discard the foil, and bake for an additional 10 to 12 minutes, or until top is browned. Allow lasagna to rest for 5 minutes, then serve immediately.

Note: The dish can be cooked up to 2 days in advance and refrigerated, tightly covered. Reheat in 350°F oven, covered, for 30 to 40 minutes.

Variation:

∗ Use any variety of meatball that is complemented by tomato sauce.

Be sure to buy the right lasagna noodles for this dish. The pre-cooked noodles are fairly new to the market, and they are what they say: noodles that are partially cooked to rid them of some of the starch, and then dehydrated. Regular lasagna noodles will not cook as well.

Italian Beef and Sausage Meatballs

The inclusion of sun-dried tomatoes and wine, herbs, and cheese gives the meatballs a hearty flavor. By using sausage in the meat mixture the complexity of the flavor is further increased. Serve them over pasta or by themselves with a tossed salad.

Makes 4 to 6 servings | Active time: 20 minutes | Start to finish: 35 minutes

½ cup sun-dried tomatoes, packed in olive oil

2 shallots, chopped

3 garlic cloves, minced

1 large egg

3 tablespoons dry red wine

½ cup seasoned Italian breadcrumbs

⅓ cup grated whole milk mozzarella

2 tablespoons chopped fresh parsley

1 tablespoon chopped fresh oregano or 1 teaspoon dried

¾ pound ground chuck

½ pound sweet or spicy bulk Italian pork sausage

Salt and freshly ground black pepper to taste

Vegetable oil spray

FOR DIPPING:

1 cup Herbed Tomato Sauce (page 21) or purchased marinara sauce, heated

1. Preheat the oven to 450°F. Line a rimmed baking sheet with heavy-duty aluminum foil, and spray the foil with vegetable oil spray. Drain sun-dried tomatoes, pressing with the back of a spoon to extract as much liquid as possible. Reserve oil, chop tomatoes finely, and set aside.

2. Heat reserved oil in a small skillet over medium-high heat. Add shallots and garlic, and cook, stirring frequently, for 3 minutes, or until shallots are translucent. While vegetables cook, whisk egg and wine in a mixing bowl, and add breadcrumbs, cheese, parsley, and oregano, and mix well.

3. Add vegetable mixture, beef, and sausage to the mixing bowl, season to taste with salt and pepper, and mix well again. Make mixture into 1½-inch meatballs, and arrange meatballs on the prepared pan. Spray tops of meatballs with vegetable oil spray.

4. Bake meatballs for 12 to 15 minutes, or until cooked through. Remove the pan from the oven, and serve immediately, accompanied by a bowl of Herbed Tomato Sauce for dipping.

Note: The meatball mixture can be prepared up to 1 day in advance and refrigerated, tightly covered. Also, the meatballs can be baked up to 2 days in advance and refrigerated, tightly covered. Reheat them in a 350°F oven, covered, for 10 to 12 minutes, or until hot.

Variation:

✳ Substitute ground chicken or turkey for all or any of the meats above.

Of all the convenience products on the market, perhaps one of the worst is minced garlic. It comes packed in both oil and water, and you should always avoid using it because the flavor isn't good. On the other hand, some supermarkets carry small packages of whole garlic cloves that are peeled. These are great, and you can use them in any recipe.

Sicilian Meatballs

The use of pine nuts and dried currants is characteristic of Sicilian cuisine; it comes from the Arabic influence from North Africa sustained in the region. The combination of Italian sausage and ground pork, with vegetables and herbs, is joined by these two special ingredients in these meatballs.

Makes 4 to 6 servings | Active time: 20 minutes | Start to finish: 45 minutes

2 tablespoons olive oil

½ small red onion, chopped

2 garlic cloves, minced

1 large egg

2 tablespoons whole milk

½ cup seasoned Italian breadcrumbs

¼ cup freshly grated Parmesan

¼ cup pine nuts, toasted

3 tablespoons dried currants

2 tablespoons chopped fresh oregano or 2 teaspoons dried

2 tablespoons chopped fresh parsley

¾ pound ground pork

½ pound sweet or spicy bulk Italian sausage

Salt and freshly ground black pepper to taste

Vegetable oil spray

2 cups Herbed Tomato Sauce (page 21) or purchased marinara sauce

1. Preheat the oven broiler. Line a rimmed baking sheet with heavy-duty aluminum foil, and spray the foil with vegetable oil spray.

2. Heat oil in a large skillet over medium-high heat. Add onion and garlic, and cook, stirring frequently, for 3 minutes, or until onion is translucent.

Combine egg and milk in a mixing bowl, and whisk until smooth. Add breadcrumbs, Parmesan, pine nuts, currants, oregano, and parsley, and mix well.

3. Add onion mixture, pork, and sausage, season to taste with salt and pepper, and mix well again. Make mixture into 1½-inch meatballs, and arrange meatballs on the prepared pan. Spray tops of meatballs with vegetable oil spray.

4. Broil meatballs 6 inches from the broiler element, turning them with tongs to brown all sides. While meatballs brown, heat Herbed Tomato Sauce in the skillet in which the vegetables were cooked.

5. Remove meatballs from the baking pan with a slotted spoon, and add meatballs to sauce. Bring to a boil, and simmer meatballs, covered, over low heat, turning occasionally with a slotted spoon, for 15 minutes. Season to taste with salt and pepper, and serve immediately.

Note: The meatball mixture can be prepared up to 1 day in advance and refrigerated, tightly covered. Also, the dish can be cooked up to 2 days in advance and refrigerated, tightly covered. Reheat in a 350°F oven, covered, for 15 to 20 minutes, or until hot.

Variation:

✳ Substitute ground chicken or turkey for all or parts of the meats used above. I do not suggest making them with all sausage meat, however, because the texture will be too lumpy.

> Pine nuts are called *piñon* in Spanish and *pignoli* in Italian, and they are sometimes found by those names in ethnic markets where they are generally less expensive.

Mediterranean Meatballs

These meatballs, made with cracked-wheat bulgur, which adds texture as well as the healthful goodness of grains, comes from the Greek islands. They are made with a combination of lamb and beef, and then poached in a spiced tomato sauce.

Makes 4 to 6 servings | *Active time: 25 minutes* | *Start to finish: 1¾ hours, including 1 hour to chill mixture*

1 large egg

⅔ cup dry red wine, divided

½ cup cracked-wheat bulgur

⅔ cup chopped fresh parsley, divided

3 scallions, white parts and 2-inches of green tops, chopped

4 garlic cloves, minced, divided

2 teaspoons ground cumin

2 teaspoons ground coriander

¾ pound ground lamb

½ pound ground beef

Salt and freshly ground black pepper to taste

¼ cup olive oil

1 medium onion, diced

1 (28-ounce) can crushed tomatoes in tomato puree

1 (3-inch) cinnamon stick

1 bay leaf

Vegetable oil spray

1. Preheat the oven broiler. Line a rimmed baking sheet with heavy-duty aluminum foil, and spray the foil with vegetable oil spray.

2. Combine egg and 2 tablespoons wine in a mixing bowl, and whisk until smooth. Add bulgur, ½ cup parsley, 2 garlic cloves, cumin, and coriander, and mix well.

3. Add lamb and beef, season to taste with salt and pepper, and knead mixture for 2 minutes. Refrigerate mixture for 1 hour.

4. While mixture chills, heat olive oil in a large skillet over medium-high heat. Add onion and remaining 2 garlic cloves, and cook, stirring frequently, for 3 minutes, or until onion is translucent. Add remaining wine, tomatoes, cinnamon stick, and bay leaf, and bring to a boil over medium-high heat, stirring occasionally. Reduce the heat to low and simmer sauce, uncovered, for 10 minutes.

5. Make mixture into 1½-inch meatballs, and arrange meatballs on the prepared pan. Spray tops of meatballs with vegetable oil spray. Broil meatballs 6 inches from the broiler element, turning them with tongs to brown all sides Remove meatballs from the baking pan with a slotted spoon, and add meatballs to sauce. Bring to a boil, and simmer meatballs, covered, over low heat, turning occasionally with a slotted spoon, for 15 minutes. Remove and discard cinnamon stick and bay leaf, season to taste with salt and pepper, and serve immediately.

Note: The meatball mixture can be prepared up to 1 day in advance and refrigerated, tightly covered. Also, the dish can be cooked up to 2 days in advance and refrigerated, tightly covered. Reheat in a 350°F oven, covered, for 15 to 20 minutes, or until hot.

Variation:
✳ Make the meatballs with buckwheat groats or couscous.

Lemony Greek Meatballs

Garlic, oregano, and lemon form almost a holy trinity in Greek cuisine, and in this case they are joined by red wine to become a simple sauce. The meat component of these meatballs is a combination of beef and lamb.

Makes 4 to 6 servings | Active time: 20 minutes | Start to finish: 35 minutes

2 tablespoons olive oil

½ small red onion, finely chopped

3 garlic cloves, minced

1 large egg

2 tablespoons whole milk

½ cup seasoned Italian breadcrumbs

¼ cup chopped fresh parsley, divided

2 tablespoons chopped fresh oregano or 2 teaspoons dried

¾ pound ground lamb

½ pound ground chuck

Salt and freshly ground black pepper to taste

1 cup dry red wine

2 tablespoons freshly squeezed lemon juice

Vegetable oil spray

1. Preheat the oven to 450°F. Line a rimmed baking sheet with heavy-duty aluminum foil, and spray the foil with vegetable oil spray.

2. Heat oil in a small skillet over medium-high heat. Add onion and garlic, and cook, stirring frequently, for 3 minutes, or until onion is translucent. While vegetables cook, whisk egg and milk in a mixing bowl, and add breadcrumbs, ½ of parsley, and oregano, and mix well.

3. Add ½ of vegetable mixture, lamb, and beef to the mixing bowl, season to taste with salt and cayenne, and mix well again. Make mixture into 1½-inch meatballs, and arrange meatballs on the prepared pan. Spray tops of meatballs with vegetable oil spray.

4. Bake meatballs for 12 to 15 minutes, or until cooked through. While meatballs bake, add wine to the skillet with remaining onion mixture, and bring to a boil over high heat, stirring occasionally. Cook until liquid is reduced by ½, then add remaining 2 tablespoons parsley and lemon juice, and cook for an additional 2 minutes, stirring occasionally. Season to taste with salt and pepper.

5. Remove the pan from the oven, and place meatballs in a shallow bowl. Pour wine mixture over meatballs, stirring to coat them well, and serve immediately.

Note: The meatball mixture can be prepared up to 1 day in advance and refrigerated, tightly covered. Also, the meatballs can be baked up to 2 days in advance and refrigerated, tightly covered. Reheat them in a 350°F oven, covered, for 10 to 12 minutes, or until hot.

Variation:

✳ Substitute ground chicken or turkey for any or all of the meats used above. If using poultry, cook with white wine rather than red.

> To reduce a sauce is like to reduce your body; it's losing weight. In this case, it's liquid that's boiled down so it loses some of its water through evaporation. This reduction, as the process is known, intensifies the flavor of the resulting liquid while shrinking its volume.

Grilled Greek Meatballs

In Greek, meatballs have a different name depending on how they're cooked. While *keftedes* are fried or grilled meatballs such as these, meatballs in a sauce are called *yuvarlakia*.

Makes 4 to 6 servings | *Active time: 20 minutes* | *Start to finish: 35 minutes*

8 to 12 (8-inch) bamboo skewers

3 tablespoons olive oil

2 shallots, chopped

3 garlic cloves, chopped

1 large egg

2 tablespoons freshly squeezed lemon juice

1 tablespoon tomato paste

½ cup seasoned Italian breadcrumbs

2 tablespoons chopped fresh parsley

2 tablespoons chopped fresh mint

1 tablespoon fresh thyme
or 1 teaspoon dried

1 tablespoon chopped fresh oregano
or 1 teaspoon dried

1 teaspoon grated lemon zest

¾ pound ground chuck

¾ pounds ground lamb

Salt and freshly ground black pepper to taste

Vegetable oil spray

FOR DIPPING:

1 cup Greek Feta Sauce (page 29) or Middle Eastern Yogurt Sauce (page 33)

1. Soak the bamboo skewers in cold water to cover. Prepare a medium-hot charcoal or gas grill, or preheat the oven broiler.

2. Heat oil in a small skillet over medium-high heat. Add shallots and garlic, and cook, stirring frequently, for 3 minutes, or until shallots are translucent. While vegetables cook, whisk egg, lemon juice, and tomato paste in a mixing bowl, and add breadcrumbs, parsley, mint, thyme, oregano, and lemon zest, and mix well.

3. Add shallot mixture, beef, and lamb to the mixing bowl, season to taste with salt and pepper, and mix well again.

4. Divide mixture into 8 to 12 portions, and form each portion into a sausage shape. Insert a skewer into each sausage so that the tip of the skewer is almost at the top of the meat.

5. Grill skewers for a total of 6 to 8 minutes, uncovered if using a charcoal grill, turning them gently with tongs to cook all sides. Serve immediately, accompanied by a bowl of Greek Feta Sauce for dipping.

Note: The meatball mixture can be prepared up to 1 day in advance and refrigerated, tightly covered. Also, the skewers can be grilled up to 2 days in advance and refrigerated, tightly covered. Reheat them in a 350°F oven, covered, for 10 to 12 minutes, or until hot.

Variation:

✱ Substitute ground chicken or turkey for any or all of the meats above.

Many recipes call for just one tablespoon of tomato paste, so I buy tomato paste in a tube. It keeps in the refrigerator for a long time. If you do open a can, freeze the remaining paste in one-tablespoon portions in an ice cube tray. Then store the small cubes in a heavy plastic bag up to six months.

Swedish Meatballs

Allspice and nutmeg, in addition to a combination of meats and a creamed sauce, are what defines the quintessential Swedish meatball, called *köttbullar* in Sweden.

Makes 4 to 6 servings | *Active time: 20 minutes* | *Start to finish: 45 minutes*

4 tablespoons (½ stick) unsalted butter, divided

1 small onion, chopped

¼ cup milk

1 large egg

1 large egg yolk

3 slices fresh white bread

¼ teaspoon ground allspice

¼ teaspoon freshly grated nutmeg

Pinch ground ginger

¾ pound ground pork

½ pound ground chuck

Salt and freshly ground black pepper to taste

¼ cup all-purpose flour

2½ cups Beef Stock (page 197) or purchased beef stock

½ cup heavy cream

Vegetable oil spray

1. Preheat the oven broiler. Line a rimmed baking sheet with heavy-duty aluminum foil, and spray the foil with vegetable oil spray.

2. Heat 2 tablespoons butter in a large skillet over medium-high heat. Add onion, and cook, stirring frequently, for 3 minutes, or until onion is translucent. Combine milk, egg, and egg yolk in a mixing bowl, and whisk until smooth.

Break bread into tiny pieces and add to mixing bowl along with allspice, nutmeg, and ginger, and mix well.

3. Add onion, pork, and beef, season to taste with salt and pepper, and mix well again. Make mixture into 1½-inch meatballs, and arrange meatballs on the prepared pan. Spray tops of meatballs with vegetable oil spray.

4. Broil meatballs 6 inches from the broiler element, turning them with tongs to brown all sides. While meatballs brown, add remaining butter to the skillet and heat over low heat. Stir flour into the skillet, and cook over low heat for 2 minutes, stirring constantly. Raise the heat to medium-high, whisk in stock and cream, and bring to a boil over medium-high heat, whisking constantly.

5. Remove meatballs from the baking pan with a slotted spoon, and add meatballs to sauce. Bring to a boil, and simmer meatballs, covered, over low heat, turning occasionally with a slotted spoon, for 15 minutes. Season to taste with salt and pepper, and serve immediately.

Note: The meatball mixture can be prepared up to 1 day in advance and refrigerated, tightly covered. Also, the dish can be cooked up to 2 days in advance and refrigerated, tightly covered. Reheat in a 350°F oven, covered, for 15 to 20 minutes, or until hot.

Variations:

✳ Substitute ground chicken or turkey for any or all of the meats used above.

✳ Add ¼ cup chopped fresh dill to the sauce.

Nutmeg is the seed of a tropical evergreen native to the Spice Islands that was most popular with European aristocracy beginning in the fifteenth century. When the fruit of the tree is split, it reveals the inch-long nutmeg seed surrounded by a lacy membrane that is ground into mace, a spice similar in flavor.

Scandinavian Dill Meatballs

These Scandinavian meatballs are prepared with fresh dill, sharp mustard, and spices. As described below, serve them with a dipping sauce containing sour cream and the same flavors.

Makes 4 to 6 servings | Active time: 15 minutes | Start to finish: 30 minutes

1 large egg

¾ cup sour cream, divided

1 tablespoon mayonnaise

3 slices seeded rye bread, broken in small pieces

⅓ cup chopped dill, divided

3 tablespoons Dijon mustard, divided

2 scallions, white parts and 2 inches of green tops, chopped

Pinch ground allspice

Pinch ground nutmeg

¾ pound ground pork

½ pound ground veal

Salt and freshly ground black pepper to taste

Vegetable oil spray

1. Preheat the oven to 450°F. Line a rimmed baking sheet with heavy-duty aluminum foil, and spray the foil with vegetable oil spray.

2. Whisk egg, ¼ cup sour cream, and mayonnaise a mixing bowl. Add bread, 2 tablespoons dill, 1 tablespoon mustard, scallions, allspice, and nutmeg, and mix well.

3. Add pork and veal to the mixing bowl, season to taste with salt and pepper, and mix well again. Make mixture into 1½-inch meatballs, and arrange meatballs on the prepared pan. Spray tops of meatballs with vegetable oil spray.

4. Bake meatballs for 12 to 15 minutes, or until cooked through. While meatballs bake, combine remaining sour cream, remaining dill, and remaining mustard in a small bowl, and whisk well.

5. Remove the pan from the oven, and serve immediately, accompanied by the bowl of sauce for dipping.

Note: The meatball mixture can be prepared up to 1 day in advance and refrigerated, tightly covered. Also, the meatballs can be baked up to 2 days in advance and refrigerated, tightly covered. Reheat them in a 350°F oven, covered, for 10 to 12 minutes, or until hot.

Variation:

＊ Substitute ground chicken or turkey for any or all of the meats used above.

> If using white bread or bread crumbs instead of rye bread, add a teaspoon or two of caraway seeds to the meat mixture. Rye bread adds caraway flavor as well as texture.

Spanish Meatballs in Tomato-Garlic Sauce

Small meatballs in tomato sauce are one of the traditional small bites served at Spanish tapas bars. I like them accompanied by dry sherry as they do in Spain. You can serve these as a hors d'oeuvre or over some pasta for dinner with a tossed salad.

Makes 4 to 6 servings | Active time: 20 minutes | Start to finish: 50 minutes

¼ cup olive oil

1 large onion, finely chopped

1 large red bell pepper, seeds and ribs removed, and finely chopped

6 garlic cloves, minced

1 large egg

½ cup dry red wine, divided

½ cup plain breadcrumbs

⅓ cup chopped fresh parsley, divided

2 tablespoons smoked Spanish paprika

¾ pound ground chuck

¾ pound ground pork

Salt and freshly ground black pepper to taste

1 (28-ounce) can crushed tomatoes in tomato puree

1 tablespoon dried oregano

Vegetable oil spray

1. Preheat the oven broiler. Line a rimmed baking sheet with heavy-duty aluminum foil, and spray the foil with vegetable oil spray.

2. Heat oil in a large skillet over medium-high heat. Add onion, bell pepper, and garlic, and cook, stirring frequently, for 3 minutes, or until onion is translucent. Combine egg and 3 tablespoons wine in a mixing bowl, and whisk until smooth. Add breadcrumbs, ¼ cup parsley, and paprika, and mix well.

3. Add ½ of onion mixture, beef, and pork, season to taste with salt and pepper, and mix well again. Make mixture into 1½-inch meatballs, and arrange meatballs on the prepared pan. Spray tops of meatballs with vegetable oil spray.

4. Broil meatballs 6-inches from the broiler element, turning them with tongs to brown all sides. While meatballs brown, add remaining wine, tomatoes, and oregano to the skillet with remaining onion mixture. Bring to a boil over medium-high heat, stirring occasionally, then reduce the heat to medium, and simmer sauce, uncovered, for 10 minutes.

5. Remove meatballs from the baking pan with a slotted spoon, and add meatballs to sauce. Bring to a boil, and simmer meatballs, covered, over low heat, turning occasionally with a slotted spoon, for 15 minutes. Season to taste with salt and pepper, and serve immediately.

Note: The meatball mixture can be prepared up to 1 day in advance and refrigerated, tightly covered. Also, the dish can be cooked up to 2 days in advance and refrigerated, tightly covered. Reheat in a 350°F oven, covered, for 15 to 20 minutes, or until hot.

Variation:
∗ Substitute ground chicken or turkey for any or all of the meats. If using poultry, substitute white wine for the red wine.

Spinach-Parmesan Meatballs

While you can serve these on top of spaghetti with more sauce, I make them cocktail size for hors d'oeuvres and use the sauce for dipping.

Makes 4 to 6 servings | *Active time: 20 minutes* | *Start to finish: 35 minutes*

2 tablespoons olive oil

2 shallots, chopped

2 garlic cloves, minced

1 celery rib, finely chopped

½ (10-ounce) package frozen chopped spinach, thawed and squeezed dry

1 large egg

2 tablespoons whole milk

½ cup seasoned Italian breadcrumbs

⅓ cup freshly grated Parmesan

2 tablespoons chopped fresh parsley

2 tablespoons chopped fresh oregano or 2 teaspoons dried

1¼ pounds meatloaf mix (or some proportion of ground pork, veal, and beef)

Salt and crushed red pepper flakes to taste

Vegetable oil spray

FOR DIPPING:

1 cup Herbed Tomato Sauce (page 21) or purchased marinara sauce, heated

1. Preheat the oven to 450°F. Line a rimmed baking sheet with heavy-duty aluminum foil, and spray the foil with vegetable oil spray.

2. Heat oil in a small skillet over medium-high heat. Add shallots, garlic, and celery, and cook, stirring frequently, for 3 minutes, or until shallots are translucent. Add spinach to the skillet, and continue to cook, stirring frequently, for 2 minutes.

3. While vegetables cook, whisk egg and milk in a mixing bowl, and add breadcrumbs, Parmesan, parsley, and oregano, and mix well.

4. Add vegetable mixture and meat to the mixing bowl, season to taste with salt and red pepper flakes, and mix well again. Make mixture into 1½-inch meatballs, and arrange meatballs on the prepared pan. Spray tops of meatballs with vegetable oil spray.

5. Bake meatballs for 12 to 15 minutes, or until cooked through. Remove the pan from the oven, and serve immediately, accompanied by a bowl of Herbed Tomato Sauce for dipping.

Note: The meatball mixture can be prepared up to 1 day in advance and refrigerated, tightly covered. Also, the meatballs can be baked up to 2 days in advance and refrigerated, tightly covered. Reheat them in a 350°F oven, covered, for 10 to 12 minutes, or until hot.

Variation:

✳ Substitute ground chicken or turkey for all or any of the meats above.

> The amount of water that comes out of a thawed package of frozen spinach is amazing. It's important to press out as much liquid as possible, or the spinach will be soupy and not sauté well.

Chapter 7

Cluck and Gobble:
Meatballs with Chicken and Turkey

*F*amed nineteenth-century French gastronome Jean Anthelme Brillat-Savarin once wrote that "poultry is for the cook what canvas is for the painter." Its inherently mild flavor takes to many methods of seasoning, and poultry is relatively quick to cook.

Ground chicken and turkey are relatively new on the market and have become increasingly popular as people cut back on saturated fat in their diets. Ground chicken and turkey are interchangeable in this chapter's recipes. If I suggest one rather than the other that's based purely on personal preference.

Because these foods are somewhat new, many of the recipes that utilize them—including some in this chapter—are adaptations from other meats, most noticeably pork, which has an equally delicate flavor. So in addition to these recipes, look at those in Chapter 4; any recipe made with ground pork (rather than sausage or ham) can also be made with chicken and turkey.

Herbed Turkey Meatballs

Fresh apple adds moisture as well as a slightly sweet flavor to these lean meatballs flavored with a variety of herbs and spices. Serve them with potato salad during the summer or some mashed potatoes during colder months.

Makes 4 to 6 servings | Active time: 15 minutes | Start to finish: 30 minutes

1 large egg

2 tablespoons whole milk

½ cup plain breadcrumbs

¼ cup grated Monterey Jack cheese

1 Golden Delicious or Granny Smith apple, peeled, cored, and grated

3 tablespoons chopped fresh sage or 1 tablespoon dried

2 tablespoons chopped fresh parsley

1 tablespoon fresh thyme or 1 teaspoon dried

Pinch of ground allspice

1¼ pounds ground turkey

Salt and freshly ground black pepper to taste

Vegetable oil spray

FOR DIPPING:

1 cup Southern Barbecue Sauce (page 23) or commercial barbecue sauce, heated

1. Preheat the oven to 450°F. Line a rimmed baking sheet with heavy-duty aluminum foil, and spray the foil with vegetable oil spray.

2. Whisk egg and milk in a mixing bowl, and add breadcrumbs, cheese, apple, sage, parsley, thyme, and allspice, and mix well. Add turkey, season to taste with salt and pepper, and mix well again. Make mixture into 1½-inch meatballs, and arrange meatballs on the prepared pan. Spray tops of meatballs with vegetable oil spray.

3. Bake meatballs for 12 to 15 minutes, or until cooked through and no longer pink. Remove the pan from the oven, and serve immediately, accompanied by a bowl of Southern Barbecue Sauce for dipping.

Note: The meatball mixture can be prepared up to 1 day in advance and refrigerated, tightly covered. Also, the meatballs can be baked up to 2 days in advance and refrigerated, tightly covered. Reheat them in a 350°F oven, covered, for 10 to 12 minutes, or until hot.

Variation:

* Make the meatballs with ground pork, ground veal, or some combination of the two.

Chicken Croquettes

Croquettes of all types are a way to stretch leftovers. Chopped food is folded into a thick white sauce, formed into balls, and fried. They are very easy to make.

Makes 4 to 6 servings | Active time: 20 minutes | Start to finish: 1½ hours, including 1 hour to chill mixture

4 tablespoons (½ stick) unsalted butter

2 shallot, finely chopped

1 cup all-purpose flour, divided

⅔ cup milk

⅔ cup chicken stock

3 cups finely chopped cooked chicken

2 tablespoons chopped fresh parsley

1 tablespoon Cajun seasoning

2 large eggs, lightly beaten

1 cup plain breadcrumbs

3 cups vegetable oil for frying

FOR DIPPING:

1 cup Herbed Tomato Sauce (page 21), heated, or Creamy Chipotle Sauce (page 27)

1. Heat butter in a saucepan over medium heat. Add shallots and cook, stirring frequently, for 2 minutes. Add ⅓ cup flour, reduce the heat to low, and cook for 2 minutes, stirring constantly. Whisk in milk and stock, and bring to a boil over medium heat, whisking constantly. Reduce the heat to low, and simmer sauce for 2 minutes. Remove the pan from the heat.

2. Stir chicken, parsley, and Cajun seasoning into sauce, and transfer mixture to a 9x13-inch baking pan. Spread mixture evenly, and refrigerate for 30 minutes or until cold, loosely covered with plastic wrap.

3. Place remaining flour on a sheet of plastic wrap, combine egg and 2 tablespoons water in a shallow bowl, and place breadcrumbs on another sheet of plastic wrap. With wet hands, form mixture into 2-inch balls. Dust balls with flour, dip into egg mixture, and dip into breadcrumbs, pressing to ensure crumbs adhere. Refrigerate balls for 30 minutes.

4. Heat oil in a saucepan over medium-high heat to 375°F. Add croquettes, being careful not to crowd the pan. Cook croquettes for a total of 3 to 5 minutes, or until browned. Remove croquettes from the pan with a slotted spoon, and drain well on paper towels. Serve immediately, accompanied by a bowl of Herbed Tomato Sauce or Creamy Chipotle Sauce for dipping.

Note: The croquettes can be prepared for frying up to 1 day in advance and refrigerated, tightly covered. They can also be fried in advance; reheat them in a 375°F oven for 10 to 12 minutes or until hot and crusty again.

Variations:

✳ Replace the chicken with turkey.

✳ Use chopped ham, omitting the Cajun seasoning and adding 1 tablespoon chopped fresh sage, salt, and pepper.

✳ Use chopped fish or seafood— salmon, cod, halibut, shrimp, and crab all work well—and replace the Cajun seasoning with 1 tablespoon Old Bay seasoning.

As a general rule, the thinner the layer of food, the faster it chills. That's why this croquette mixture is transferred to a baking pan rather than being chilled in a saucepan. For large quantities of liquid like soups or stews, portion them into pint and quart containers to speed chilling.

Chicken Meatballs Piccata

Boil some potatoes or have a crusty baguette on hand, because you're going to want to savor every drop of this luscious lemony sauce dotted with tangy capers. Serve with a light, dry white wine and a tossed salad.

Makes 4 to 6 servings | *Active time: 20 minutes* | *Start to finish: 50 minutes*

2 tablespoons olive oil

1 small onion, chopped

3 garlic cloves, minced

1 large egg

2 tablespoons whole milk

½ cup seasoned Italian breadcrumbs

½ cup chopped fresh parsley, divided

1 teaspoon Italian seasoning

1¼ pounds ground chicken

Salt and freshly ground black pepper to taste

2 tablespoons unsalted butter

3 tablespoons all-purpose flour

1½ cups chicken stock

⅓ cup freshly squeezed lemon juice

¼ cup small capers, drained and rinsed

Vegetable oil spray

1. Preheat the oven broiler. Line a rimmed baking sheet with heavy-duty aluminum foil, and spray the foil with vegetable oil spray.

2. Heat oil in a large skillet over medium-high heat. Add onion and garlic, and cook, stirring frequently, for 3 minutes, or until onion is translucent. While vegetables cook, whisk egg and milk in a mixing bowl, add breadcrumbs, 2 tablespoons parsley, and Italian seasoning, and mix well.

3. Add ½ of vegetable mixture and chicken to the mixing bowl, season to taste with salt and pepper, and mix well again. Make mixture into 1½-inch meatballs, and arrange meatballs on the prepared pan. Spray tops of meatballs with vegetable oil spray.

4. Broil meatballs 6 inches from the broiler element, turning them with tongs to brown all sides.

5. While meatballs brown, add butter to the vegetables remaining in the skillet over medium-high heat. Reduce the heat to low, stir in flour and cook, stirring constantly, for 2 minutes. Whisk in stock, and lemon juice, and bring to a boil over medium-high heat, whisking constantly. Stir in remaining parsley and capers, and simmer 3 minutes, uncovered.

6. Remove meatballs from the baking pan with a slotted spoon, and add meatballs to sauce. Bring to a boil, and simmer meatballs, covered, over low heat, turning occasionally with a slotted spoon, for 15 minutes or until meatballs are cooked through and no longer pink. Serve immediately.

Note: The chicken mixture can be prepared up to 1 day in advance and refrigerated, tightly covered. Also, the dish can be cooked up to 2 days in advance and refrigerated, tightly covered. Reheat it in a 350°F oven, covered, for 15 to 20 minutes, or until hot.

Variations:

* Replace the chicken with ground pork or ground veal.
* Substitute freshly squeezed lime juice for the lemon juice.

To get the maximum amount of juice from citrus fruits, roll them back and forth on a counter or prick the skin and microwave them on high power for 30 seconds.

Chicken Meatballs Cacciatore

Cacciatore is Italian for "hunter's style." Any number of dishes from chicken to beef to veal can use cacciatore as a description, but all it means is that the dish is cooked with tomatoes, and frequently with wild mushrooms as well. The rest of the ingredients are up to the cook. This dish contains both dried porcini mushrooms and chopped prosciutto for flavor.

Makes 4 to 6 servings | Active time: 25 minutes | Start to finish: 55 minutes

½ ounce dried porcini mushrooms

1 cup boiling chicken stock

3 tablespoons olive oil

¼ pound prosciutto, finely chopped

1 large onion, chopped

4 garlic cloves, minced

½ pound mushrooms, wiped with a damp paper towel, and sliced

1 (28-ounce) can diced tomatoes, undrained

¼ cup chopped fresh parsley, divided

1 teaspoon Italian seasoning

1 bay leaf

1 large egg

2 tablespoons whole milk

½ cup seasoned Italian breadcrumbs

¼ cup freshly grated Parmesan

1¼ pounds ground chicken

Salt and freshly ground black pepper to taste

Vegetable oil spray

1. Soak porcini in boiling stock for 10 minutes. Drain, reserving soaking liquid. Discard stems and finely chop mushrooms. Set aside. Strain liquid through a paper coffee filter or paper towel. Reserve mushrooms and liquid.

2. While mushrooms soak, heat olive oil in large skillet over medium-high heat. Add prosciutto, onion, and garlic. Cook, stirring frequently, for 3 minutes, or until onion is translucent. Add mushrooms, and cook for 2 minutes, stirring frequently. Add chopped porcini, stock, tomatoes, 2 tablespoons parsley, Italian seasoning, and bay leaf to the pan. Bring to a boil, and cook over low heat, uncovered, for 10 minutes.

3. Preheat the oven broiler. Line a rimmed baking sheet with heavy-duty aluminum foil, and spray the foil with vegetable oil spray. Combine egg and milk in a mixing bowl, and whisk until smooth. Add breadcrumbs, Parmesan, and remaining parsley, and mix well. Add chicken, and season to taste with salt and pepper. Make mixture into 1½-inch meatballs, and arrange meatballs on the prepared pan. Spray tops of meatballs with vegetable oil spray.

4. Broil meatballs 6 inches from the broiler element, turning them with tongs to brown all sides. Remove meatballs from the baking pan with a slotted spoon, and add meatballs to sauce. Bring to a boil, and simmer meatballs, covered, over low heat, turning occasionally with a slotted spoon, for 15 minutes or until meatballs are cooked through and no longer pink. Season to taste with salt and pepper, and serve immediately.

Note: The chicken mixture can be prepared up to 1 day in advance and refrigerated, tightly covered. Also, the dish can be cooked up to 2 days in advance and refrigerated, tightly covered. Reheat it in a 350°F oven, covered, for 15 to 20 minutes, or until hot.

Variations:
* Replace the chicken with ground chuck for a heartier dish.
* Substitute some Italian pork sausage for some of the ground turkey.

Turkey and Basil Meatballs

I frequently make these meatballs during the summer when basil is bountiful in my garden.

Makes 4 to 6 servings | Active time: 20 minutes | Start to finish: 35 minutes

2 tablespoons olive oil

2 shallots, chopped

2 garlic cloves, minced

1 cup mayonnaise

1 cup tightly packed chopped fresh basil

¼ cup chopped fresh parsley

¼ cup small capers, drained and rinsed

2 garlic cloves, minced

1 large shallot, chopped

2 teaspoons herbes de Provence

Salt and freshly ground black pepper to taste

1 large egg

½ cup plain breadcrumbs

1¼ pounds ground turkey

Vegetable oil spray

Fresh parsley for garnish

1. Preheat the oven to 450°F. Line a rimmed baking sheet with heavy-duty aluminum foil, and spray the foil with vegetable oil spray.

2. Heat oil in a small skillet over medium-high heat. Add shallots and garlic, and cook, stirring frequently, for 3 minutes, or until shallots are translucent. Combine shallot mixture, mayonnaise, basil, parsley, capers, garlic, shallot, herbes de Provence, salt, and pepper in a mixing bowl, and stir well.

3. Whisk egg, ½ cup basil-mayonnaise mixture, and breadcrumbs in a mixing bowl, and mix well. Add turkey to the mixing bowl, season to taste with salt and pepper, and mix well again. Make mixture into 1½-inch meatballs, and arrange meatballs on the prepared pan. Spray tops of meatballs with vegetable oil spray.

4. Bake meatballs for 12 to 15 minutes, or until cooked through and no longer pink. Remove the pan from the oven, and serve immediately, accompanied by a bowl of remaining basil sauce for dipping. Garnish with fresh parsley, if desired.

Note: The turkey mixture can be prepared up to 1 day in advance and refrigerated, tightly covered. Also, the meatballs can be baked up to 2 days in advance and refrigerated, tightly covered. Reheat them in a 350°F oven, covered, for 10 to 12 minutes, or until hot.

Variations:

* Replace the turkey with ground pork or ground veal.
* Substitute some chopped fresh oregano for some of the basil.

Basil has been used in the kitchen as early as 400 BCE when Greek botanist Chrysippos described it as one of his favorite seasonings. The Romans used it in their bouquet garni, and the Byzantines used it to flavor sauces.

Sun-Dried Tomato and Herb Chicken Meatballs

Sun-dried tomatoes are one of my favorite ingredients; the process intensifies the natural sugars and succulent flavor. These meatballs, perfect as a hors d'oeuvre, also contain a variety of fresh herbs and some creamy mozzarella.

Makes 4 to 6 servings | *Active time: 20 minutes* | *Start to finish: 35 minutes*

⅔ cup sun-dried tomatoes packed in olive oil

1 medium onion, chopped

2 garlic cloves, minced

1 celery rib, chopped

1 large egg

2 tablespoons whole milk

½ cup seasoned Italian breadcrumbs

½ cup grated whole milk mozzarella

2 tablespoons chopped fresh parsley

2 tablespoons chopped fresh rosemary or 2 teaspoons dried

1 tablespoon chopped fresh oregano or 1 teaspoon dried

1¼ pounds ground chicken

Salt and freshly ground black pepper to taste

Vegetable oil spray

FOR DIPPING:

1 cup Herbed Tomato Sauce (page 21) or purchased marinara sauce, heated

1. Preheat the oven to 450°F. Line a rimmed baking sheet with heavy-duty aluminum foil, and spray the foil with vegetable oil spray. Drain tomatoes, reserving oil. Finely chop tomatoes, and set aside.

2. Heat reserved oil in a medium skillet over medium-high heat. Add onion, garlic, and celery, and cook, stirring frequently, for 3 minutes, or until onion is translucent.

3. While vegetables cook, whisk egg and milk in a mixing bowl, add breadcrumbs, cheese, parsley, rosemary, and oregano, and mix well. Add onion mixture and chicken to the mixing bowl, season to taste with salt and pepper, and mix well again. Make mixture into 1½-inch meatballs, and arrange meatballs on the prepared pan. Spray tops of meatballs with vegetable oil spray.

4. Bake meatballs for 12 to 15 minutes, or until cooked through and no longer pink. Remove the pan from the oven, and serve immediately, accompanied by a bowl of Herbed Tomato Sauce for dipping.

Note: The chicken mixture can be prepared up to 1 day in advance and refrigerated, tightly covered. Also, the meatballs can be baked up to 2 days in advance and refrigerated, tightly covered. Reheat them in a 350°F oven, covered, for 10 to 12 minutes, or until hot.

Variations:

✳ Replace the chicken with ground pork or ground veal.

✳ Substitute some uncooked chicken sausage for some of the ground chicken.

Graters often become clogged when used for semi-soft cheeses like commercial mozzarella, but if you spray the holes with vegetable oil spray first, the grater should remain clear. It will be easier to clean, too.

Turkey Meatballs in Mexican Molé Sauce

There's an intensity to this classic Mexican sauce that comes from a combination of spices, ground nuts, and cocoa powder. Serve these meatballs over Mexican rice with a pile of warm tortillas on the side.

Makes 4 to 6 servings | *Active time: 15 minutes* | *Start to finish: 45 minutes*

3 tablespoons olive oil

2 onions, chopped

6 garlic cloves, minced

3 tablespoons chili powder

1 tablespoon ground cumin

2½ cups chicken stock, divided

1 (14.5-oz.) can tomatoes, drained

¼ cup peanut butter

¼ cup chopped raisins

2 tablespoons granulated sugar

2 tablespoons unsweetened cocoa powder

Salt and cayenne to taste

1 large egg

¾ cup crushed tortilla chips

1¼ pounds ground turkey

Freshly ground black pepper to taste

1. Heat oil in a large skillet over medium-high heat. Add onions and garlic and cook, stirring frequently, for 3 minutes, or until onions are translucent. Remove ⅓ of mixture, and set aside. Stir chili powder and cumin into the skillet, and cook, stirring constantly, for 1 minute.

2. Add 2¼ cups chicken stock, tomatoes, peanut butter, raisins, sugar, and cocoa powder. Stir well, and bring to a boil over high heat. Reduce the heat to low and simmer sauce, uncovered, for 20 minutes or until lightly thickened. Season to taste with salt and cayenne.

3. Preheat the oven broiler. Line a rimmed baking sheet with heavy-duty aluminum foil, and spray the foil with vegetable oil spray.

4. While sauce simmers, whisk egg and remaining ¼ cup stock in a mixing bowl, add crushed tortilla chips, and mix well. Add reserved vegetable mixture and turkey to the mixing bowl, season to taste with salt and pepper, and mix well again. Make mixture into 1½-inch meatballs, and arrange meatballs on the prepared pan. Spray tops of meatballs with vegetable oil spray.

5. Broil meatballs 6 inches from the broiler element, turning them with tongs to brown all sides. Remove meatballs from the baking pan with a slotted spoon, and add meatballs to sauce. Bring to a boil, and simmer meatballs, covered, over low heat, turning occasionally with a slotted spoon, for 15 minutes or until meatballs are cooked through and no longer pink.

Note: The turkey mixture can be prepared up to 1 day in advance and refrigerated, tightly covered. Also, the dish can be cooked up to 2 days in advance and refrigerated, tightly covered. Reheat it in a 350°F oven, covered, for 15 to 20 minutes, or until hot.

Variations:

✳ Replace the turkey with ground pork or ground veal.

✳ Substitute some uncooked chicken sausage for some of the ground turkey.

Bombay Turkey Meatballs

Chopped dried apricots add sweetness and nuts add crunch to the curry-flavored turkey meatballs, which are then topped with a yogurt-based sauce. I serve the meatballs and sauce tucked into pita bread.

Makes 4 to 6 servings | *Active time: 20 minutes* | *Start to finish: 35 minutes*

⅔ cup plain yogurt

¼ cup pine nuts

2 tablespoons vegetable oil

1 medium onion, finely chopped

2 garlic cloves, minced

1 large egg

2 tablespoons whole milk

2 slices white bread, broken into small pieces

½ cup finely chopped dried apricots

¼ cup chopped fresh cilantro

1 tablespoon curry powder

1¼ pounds ground turkey

Salt and freshly ground black pepper to taste

2 teaspoon ground cumin

1 medium tomato, rinsed, cored, seeded, and finely chopped

Vegetable oil spray

1. Preheat the oven to 450°F. Line a rimmed baking sheet with heavy-duty aluminum foil, and spray the foil with vegetable oil spray.

2. Place yogurt in a strainer set over a mixing bowl. Shake the strainer gently a few times, and allow yogurt to drain for at least 30 minutes at room temperature or up to 6 hours, refrigerated. Discard whey from the mixing bowl, and place yogurt in the bowl. Set aside.

3. While yogurt drains, place pine nuts in a small skillet over medium heat. Cook, stirring frequently, for 2 to 3 minutes, or until nuts brown. Remove nuts from the skillet with a slotted spoon, and set aside. Heat oil in the same skillet over medium-high heat. Add onion and garlic and cook, stirring frequently, for 5 minutes or until onion is soft.

4. While vegetables cook, whisk egg and milk in a mixing bowl, and add bread, dried apricots, cilantro, and curry powder, and mix well.

5. Add onion mixture and turkey to the mixing bowl, season to taste with salt and pepper, and mix well again. Make mixture into 1½-inch meatballs, and arrange meatballs on the prepared pan. Spray tops of meatballs with vegetable oil spray.

6. Bake meatballs for 12 to 15 minutes, or until cooked through and no longer pink. While meatballs bake, combine yogurt and cumin in a small bowl, and stir well. Gently fold in tomato. Remove the pan from the oven, and serve immediately, accompanied by the bowl of yogurt sauce for dipping.

Note: The turkey mixture can be prepared up to 1 day in advance and refrigerated, tightly covered. Also, the meatballs can be baked up to 2 days in advance and refrigerated, tightly covered. Reheat them in a 350°F oven, covered, for 10 to 12 minutes, or until hot.

Variations:

✳ Replace the turkey with ground pork or ground veal.

✳ Substitute some dried currants or dried cranberries for the chopped dried apricots.

Crunchy Asian Turkey Meatballs

Aromatic from heady toasted sesame oil and other Asian ingredients, these crispy balls are a great addition to any cocktail party menu. If serving them for dinner, accompany with stir-fried vegetables on the side.

Makes 4 to 6 servings | *Active time: 20 minutes* | *Start to finish: 35 minutes*

2 tablespoons Asian sesame oil

4 scallions, white parts and 3 inches of green tops, chopped

2 tablespoons grated fresh ginger

3 garlic cloves, minced

1 large egg

3 tablespoons fish sauce (nam pla)

1 cup panko breadcrumbs, divided

½ cup finely chopped water chestnuts

¼ cup chopped fresh cilantro

1¼ pounds ground turkey

Salt and red pepper flakes to taste

Vegetable oil spray

FOR DIPPING:

1 cup Thai Sweet and Spicy Dipping Sauce (page 26), Ponzu Sauce (page 25), or soy sauce

1. Preheat the oven to 450°F. Line a rimmed baking sheet with heavy-duty aluminum foil, and spray the foil with vegetable oil spray.

2. Heat sesame oil in a small skillet over medium-high heat. Add scallions, ginger, and garlic, and cook, stirring frequently, for 2 minutes, or until scallions are translucent.

3. While vegetables cook, whisk egg and fish sauce in a mixing bowl, and add ½ cup breadcrumbs, water chestnuts, and cilantro, and mix well.

4. Add vegetable mixture and turkey to the mixing bowl, season to taste with salt and red pepper flakes, and mix well again. Make mixture into 1½-inch meatballs, roll meatballs in remaining ½ cup panko, and arrange meatballs on the prepared pan. Spray tops of meatballs with vegetable oil spray.

5. Bake meatballs for 12 to 15 minutes, or until cooked through and no longer pink. Remove the pan from the oven, and serve immediately, accompanied by a bowl of Thai Sweet and Spicy Dipping Sauce or Ponzu Sauce.

Note: The meatball mixture can be prepared up to 1 day in advance and refrigerated, tightly covered. Also, the meatballs can be baked up to 2 days in advance and refrigerated, tightly covered. Reheat them in a 350°F oven, covered, for 10 to 12 minutes, or until hot.

Variations:
* Replace the turkey with ground pork or ground veal.
* Substitute cooked white rice for the panko.

Although cilantro is traditional in both Asian and Hispanic cooking, always feel free to substitute parsley.

Thai Chicken Meatballs

Aromatic lemongrass is the primary flavoring in these delicate chicken balls, made slightly spicy with both garlic and crushed red pepper flakes. But feel free to tone down the pepper; that's a matter of personal preference.

Makes 4 to 6 servings | Active time: 20 minutes | Start to finish: 35 minutes

2 stalks fresh lemongrass

4 scallions, white parts only, sliced

2 garlic cloves, peeled

1 tablespoon Asian fish sauce (nam pla)

1 tablespoon water

½ teaspoon crushed red pepper flakes or to taste

1 large egg

2 tablespoons whole milk

¾ cup cooked white rice

1¼ pounds ground chicken

Salt and freshly ground black pepper to taste

¾ cup panko breadcrumbs

Vegetable oil spray

FOR DIPPING:

1 cup Sweet and Sour Sauce (page 25) or purchased duck sauce

1. Preheat the oven to 450°F. Line a rimmed baking sheet with heavy-duty aluminum foil, and spray the foil with vegetable oil spray.

2. Remove and discard out leaves from lemongrass, and trim root end. Slice bottom 3 inches of root, and discard remainder. Combine lemongrass, scallions, garlic, fish sauce, water, and red pepper flakes in a blender, and puree until smooth. Set aside.

3. Whisk egg and milk in a mixing bowl, and add lemongrass mixture and rice, and mix well. Add chicken to the mixing bowl, season to taste with salt and pepper, and mix well again. Make mixture into 1½-inch meatballs, roll meatballs in panko, and arrange meatballs on the prepared pan. Spray tops of meatballs with vegetable oil spray.

4. Bake meatballs for 12 to 15 minutes, or until cooked through and no longer pink. Remove the pan from the oven, and serve immediately, accompanied by a bowl of Sweet and Sour Sauce.

Note: The meatball mixture can be prepared up to 1 day in advance and refrigerated, tightly covered. Also, the meatballs can be baked up to 2 days in advance and refrigerated, tightly covered. Reheat them in a 350°F oven, covered, for 10 to 12 minutes, or until hot.

Variations:

* Replace the turkey with ground pork or ground veal.
* Substitute cooked white rice for the panko.

> Lemongrass, technically an herb and used extensively in Thai and Vietnamese cooking, is characterized by a strong citrus flavor with a spicy finish similar to that of ginger. Fresh lemongrass is sold by the stalk. It looks like a pale, fibrous, woody scallion. Cut the lower bulb five inches from the stalk, discarding the fibrous upper part. Trim off the outer layers, as you would peel an onion; then bruise the stem to release the flavor. If you can't find lemongrass, substitute 1 teaspoon grated lemon zest plus 2 tablespoons lemon juice for each stalk of lemongrass specified in a recipe, along with a pinch of ginger powder.

Turkey Meatballs Tetrazzini

The combination of mushrooms and turkey in a cream sauce laced with sherry and Parmesan is irresistible and a great dish for buffet entertaining. Serve atop orzo, rice-shaped pasta.

Makes 4 to 6 servings | *Active time: 20 minutes* | *Start to finish: 50 minutes*

4 tablespoons unsalted butter, divided

2 tablespoons olive oil

2 shallots, chopped

2 garlic cloves, minced

1 celery rib, chopped

1 large egg

2 tablespoons whole milk

½ cup plain breadcrumbs

1¼ pounds ground turkey

Salt and freshly ground black pepper to taste

½ pound mushrooms, wiped with a damp paper towel and sliced

3 tablespoons all-purpose flour

½ cup medium dry sherry

1½ cups half-and-half

1 cup turkey or chicken stock

¾ cup freshly grated Parmesan

Vegetable oil spray

1. Preheat the oven broiler. Line a rimmed baking sheet with heavy-duty aluminum foil, and spray the foil with vegetable oil spray.

2. Heat 2 tablespoons butter and oil in a large skillet over medium-high heat. Add shallots, garlic, and celery, and cook, stirring frequently, for 3 minutes, or until shallots are translucent. While vegetables cook, whisk egg and milk in a mixing bowl, add breadcrumbs, and mix well.

3. Add vegetable mixture and turkey to the mixing bowl, season to taste with salt and pepper, and mix well again. Make mixture into 1½-inch meatballs, and arrange meatballs on the prepared pan. Spray tops of meatballs with vegetable oil spray.

4. Broil meatballs 6 inches from the broiler element, turning them with tongs to brown all sides.

5. While meatballs brown, heat remaining butter in the skillet over medium-high heat. Add mushrooms, and cook for 3 minutes, or until mushrooms begin to soften. Reduce the heat to low, stir in flour and cook, stirring constantly, for 2 minutes. Whisk in sherry, and bring to a boil over medium-high heat, whisking constantly. Simmer 3 minutes, then add half-and-half, stock, and Parmesan, and simmer 2 minutes.

6. Remove meatballs from the baking pan with a slotted spoon, and add meatballs to sauce. Bring to a boil, and simmer meatballs, covered, over low heat, turning occasionally with a slotted spoon, for 15 minutes or until meatballs are cooked through and no longer pink.

Note: The turkey mixture can be prepared up to 1 day in advance and refrigerated, tightly covered. Also, the dish can be cooked up to 2 days in advance and refrigerated, tightly covered. Reheat it in a 350°F oven, covered, for 15 to 20 minutes, or until hot.

Variations:

* Replace the turkey with ground pork or ground veal.

* Soak ½ cup dried porcini mushrooms in ½ cup boiling water for 10 minutes. Drain mushrooms, reserving soaking liquid. Chop mushrooms, and strain liquid through a paper coffee filter or paper towel. Add mushrooms to sauce, and use soaking liquid in place of ½ cup stock.

Basque Chicken Meatballs

The Basque region of the Pyrenees between France and Spain is known for its rustic, hearty fare. These chicken meatballs are delicate, but the seasonings in the sauce give them some punch. Serve the meatballs over pasta or a cooked grain such as farro or bulgur.

Makes 4 to 6 servings | Active time: 20 minutes | Start to finish: 1 hour

¼ cup olive oil

2 large onions, chopped

6 garlic cloves, minced

¼ pound baked ham, finely chopped

1 red bell pepper, seeds and ribs removed, and chopped

2 tablespoons smoked Spanish paprika

2 teaspoons fresh thyme
or ½ teaspoon dried

1½ cups chicken stock, divided

¾ cup dry sherry

1 (14.5-oz.) can diced tomatoes, undrained

Crushed red pepper flakes to taste

1 large egg

½ cup plain breadcrumbs

1¼ pounds ground chicken

Salt and freshly ground black pepper to taste

Vegetable oil spray

1. Heat olive oil in a large skillet over medium-high heat. Add onions and garlic, and cook, stirring frequently, for 3 minutes, or until onions are translucent. Remove ⅓ of mixture, and set aside. Add ham and red bell pepper, and cook for 3 minutes, stirring frequently. Stir in paprika and thyme and cook for 1 minute, stirring constantly.

2. Add 1¼ cups stock, sherry, tomatoes, and red pepper flakes. Bring to a boil and simmer sauce, uncovered, for 15 minutes, stirring occasionally.

3. Preheat the oven broiler. Line a rimmed baking sheet with heavy-duty aluminum foil, and spray the foil with vegetable oil spray.

4. While sauce simmers, whisk egg and remaining stock in a mixing bowl, add breadcrumbs, and mix well. Add reserved vegetable mixture and chicken to the mixing bowl, season to taste with salt and pepper, and mix well again. Make mixture into 1½-inch meatballs, and arrange meatballs on the prepared pan. Spray tops of meatballs with vegetable oil spray.

5. Broil meatballs 6 inches from the broiler element, turning them with tongs to brown all sides. Remove meatballs from the baking pan with a slotted spoon, and add meatballs to sauce. Bring to a boil, and simmer meatballs, covered, over low heat, turning occasionally with a slotted spoon, for 15 minutes or until meatballs are cooked through and no longer pink.

Note: The chicken mixture can be prepared up to 1 day in advance and refrigerated, tightly covered. Also, the dish can be cooked up to 2 days in advance and refrigerated, tightly covered. Reheat it in a 350°F oven, covered, for 15 to 20 minutes, or until hot.

Variations:
* Replace the chicken with ground pork, ground veal, or ground chuck.
* Substitute some uncooked chicken sausage for some of the ground chicken.

The way you treat garlic determines the intensity of its flavor. Pushing the cloves through a garlic press is the way to extract the most punch. Mincing the cloves once they're peeled produces a milder flavor.

Chapter 8

Aquatic Adventures:

Meatballs with Fish and Seafood

There's no question from increasing consumption figures that Americans are now eating more fish and seafood, both at home and at restaurants.

With the exception of pre-minced clams, chopping fish and seafood is the responsibility of the cook, but it's an easy task with a food processor. Once cubes of fillet are partially frozen they can be chopped in a matter of seconds. In fact, there's one corner of my dishwasher reserved for the food processor work bowl because I use it so often.

While it might take more time to create the mixtures from which the fish and seafood balls are made, they do not require any pre-browning so the total amount of cooking time is shorter.

Fried Chinese Shrimp Balls

These crunchy balls are similar to the topping on shrimp toast found on Chinese-American restaurant menus. They are light and fluffy and a perfect hors d'oeuvre for a party.

Makes 4 to 6 servings | *Active time: 20 minutes* | *Start to finish: 50 minutes, including 30 minutes to chill mixture*

1½ pounds large raw shrimp (21 to 30 per pound), peeled and deveined

2 large egg whites

2 tablespoons cornstarch

½ cup chopped water chestnuts

3 scallions, white parts and 2-inches of green tops, chopped

2 tablespoons grated fresh ginger

2 tablespoons dry sherry

1 tablespoon soy sauce

1 tablespoon Asian sesame oil

Salt and freshly ground black pepper to taste

1½ cups panko breadcrumbs

3 cups vegetable oil for frying

FOR DIPPING:

1 cup Sweet and Sour Sauce (page 25) or purchased sweet and sour sauce

1. Finely chop ½ pound shrimp, and place in a mixing bowl. Puree remaining 1 pound shrimp, egg whites, and cornstarch in a food processor. Add to the mixing bowl, along with water chestnuts, scallions, ginger, sherry, soy sauce, sesame oil, salt, and pepper, and mix well. Allow mixture to chill for a minimum of 30 minutes.

2. Place panko in a shallow bowl. Make mixture into 1-inch balls, and roll balls in breadcrumbs, pressing gently so crumbs adhere.

3. Heat oil in a saucepan over medium-high heat to a temperature of 375°F. Add shrimp balls, being careful not to crowd the pan. Cook shrimp balls for a total of 2 to 3 minutes, or until browned. Remove shrimp balls from the pan with a slotted spoon, and drain well on paper towels. Serve immediately, accompanied by a bowl of Sweet and Sour Sauce for dipping.

Note: The shrimp balls can be prepared for frying up to 1 day in advance and refrigerated, tightly covered. They can also be fried in advance; reheat them in a 400°F oven for 5 to 7 minutes, or until hot and crusty again.

Variation:

* Substitute scallops or any firm-fleshed white fish like cod or tilapia for the shrimp.

To devein shrimp means to remove the black vein, actually the intestinal tract. To do this, hold the shrimp in one hand with the curved side up. Slice down the middle of the back with a paring knife, and pull out the black vein if one is present. This can also be done with a specialized tool called a deveiner.

Southwestern Crab Balls

This recipe is a variation on traditional crab cakes, with the addition of cilantro and other seasonings. You can also make them into larger patties and serve them on buns like hamburgers.

Makes 4 to 6 servings | *Active time: 20 minutes* | *Start to finish: 35 minutes*

1 pound lump crab meat

3 tablespoons unsalted butter

4 scallions, white parts and 2 inches of green tops, chopped

½ red bell pepper, seeds and ribs removed, and chopped

2 garlic cloves, minced

⅓ cup mayonnaise

1 large egg

3 tablespoons chopped fresh cilantro

1 tablespoon paprika

1 tablespoon chili powder

2 teaspoons Worcestershire sauce

½ teaspoon dried thyme

Salt and cayenne to taste

½ cup plain breadcrumbs

Vegetable oil spray

FOR DIPPING:

1 cup Creamy Chipotle Sauce (page 27) or purchased refrigerated salsa or guacamole

1. Preheat the oven to 425°F. Line a rimmed baking sheet with heavy-duty aluminum foil, and spray the foil with vegetable oil spray. Place crab on a dark surface and pick it over carefully to discard all shell fragments. Set aside.

2. Heat butter in a small skillet over medium-high heat. Add scallions, bell pepper, and garlic, and cook, stirring frequently, for 3 to 5 minutes, or until vegetables are soft. Set aside.

3. Combine mayonnaise, egg, cilantro, paprika, chili powder, Worcestershire sauce, thyme, salt, and cayenne in a mixing bowl, and whisk well. Stir in breadcrumbs, and then gently fold in crab.

4. Make mixture into 1½-inch balls, and arrange crab balls on the prepared pan. Spray tops of crab balls with vegetable oil spray. Bake crab balls for 12 to 15 minutes, or until cooked through. Remove the pan from the oven, and serve immediately, accompanied by a bowl of Creamy Chipotle Sauce for dipping.

Note: The crab mixture can be prepared up to 1 day in advance and refrigerated, tightly covered. Also, the crab balls can be baked up to 2 days in advance and refrigerated, tightly covered. Reheat them in a 350°F oven, uncovered, for 8 to 10 minutes, or until hot.

Variations:

✳ In addition to cooked fish or seafood of any kind, try cooked and finely chopped chicken or pork.

✳ Substitute 3 (6-ounce) cans of tuna fish, drained and flaked.

Picked-over crabmeat from the seafood department is a time-saver, but it's far from perfect. The best way to ensure that no shell fragments find their way into a dish is to spread out the crab on a dark-colored plate. Any bits of shell can easily be picked up against the dark background. Rub the morsels between your fingers, being careful not to break up large lumps, for any additional bits.

Gefilte Fish Balls

Gefilte fish dates from the Middle Ages in Germany, where it was conceived as way to stretch fresh fish to feed a crowd. It's served at many Jewish holidays, and it's always made from freshwater, rather than saltwater, fish.

Makes 4 to 6 servings | Active time: 45 minutes | Start to finish: 4½ hours, including 2 hours to chill mixture

1½ pounds fish fillets, some combination of whitefish, carp, and pike

3 large eggs

2 large onions, peeled, divided

2 celery ribs, divided

3 carrots, divided

½ cup matzo meal

Salt and freshly ground black pepper to taste

2 quarts fish stock or water

FOR SERVING:

½ cup prepared red or white horseradish

1. Rinse fish and pat dry with paper towels, and cut into 1-inch pieces. Place fish cubes on a sheet of plastic wrap, and freeze for 20 to 30 minutes, or until firm but not solid. Chop fish in a food processor using on-and-off pulsing.

2. Whisk eggs in a mixing bowl, and add chopped fish. Grate ½ onion, and finely chop 1 celery rib and 1 carrot. Add vegetables to mixing bowl along with matzo meal, salt, and pepper, and mix well. Refrigerate mixture for at least 2 hours, or up to 12 hours.

3. Place fish stock in a stockpot, season to taste with salt and pepper, and bring to a boil over medium-high heat. Slice remaining onion, celery, and carrots, and add vegetables to the pan.

4. Make fish mixture into 8 to 12 balls, and gently lower them into simmering stock using a slotted spoon. Bring to boil, then reduce the heat to low, cover the pan, and simmer fish for 1½ hours; add more fish stock or water if necessary to keep fish balls covered.

5. Remove fish balls and carrot slices from the pan, and allow to cool to room temperature. Refrigerate fish balls and carrots, tightly covered with plastic wrap, until very cold. Serve chilled with horseradish, with fish balls topped with carrot slices.

Note: The fish mixture can be prepared up to 1 day in advance and refrigerated, tightly covered. The dish can be prepared up to 3 days in advance, and refrigerated, tightly covered.

Variations:
* Add ¼ cup chopped dill to the fish mixture.
* Add 2 garlic cloves, minced, to the fish mixture.

There are a few noted exceptions to the current situation that fish does not come pre-chopped. One is pre-minced clams and conch, and the other—if you live in a Jewish neighborhood—is a pre-ground mixture of fin fish for making gefilte fish around such holidays as Rosh Hashana and Passover.

Italian Cod Balls

This recipe is actually more Italian-American than authentically Italian. The addition of spinach and cheeses to the cod base gives the balls flavor and few calories. Serve these on top of spaghetti.

Makes 4 to 6 servings | *Active time: 20 minutes* | *Start to finish: 50 minutes*

1¼ pounds cod fillet

1 large egg

2 tablespoons whole milk

1 cup seasoned Italian breadcrumbs, divided

¼ cup grated whole milk mozzarella

3 tablespoons freshly grated Parmesan

3 tablespoons chopped fresh parsley

1 tablespoon chopped fresh oregano or 1 teaspoon dried

½ (10-ounce) package frozen chopped spinach, thawed

Salt and freshly ground black pepper to taste

Vegetable oil spray

FOR DIPPING:

1 cup Herbed Tomato Sauce (page 21) or purchased marinara sauce, heated

1. Rinse cod, pat dry with paper towels, and cut into 1-inch pieces. Place cod cubes on a sheet of plastic wrap, and freeze for 20 to 30 minutes, or until firm but not frozen solid.

2. Preheat the oven to 425°F. Line a rimmed baking sheet with heavy-duty aluminum foil, and spray the foil with vegetable oil spray.

3. Whisk egg and milk in a mixing bowl, add ½ cup breadcrumbs, mozzarella cheese, Parmesan, parsley, and oregano, and mix well. Chop cod in a food processor using on-and-off pulsing. Add cod and spinach, season to taste with salt and pepper, and mix well again.

4. Make mixture into 1½-inch balls, roll balls in remaining breadcrumbs, and arrange cod balls on the prepared pan. Spray tops of cod balls with vegetable oil spray.

5. Bake cod balls for 12 to 15 minutes, or until cooked through. Remove the pan from the oven, and serve immediately, accompanied by a bowl of Herbed Tomato Sauce for dipping.

Note: The cod mixture can be prepared up to 1 day in advance and refrigerated, tightly covered. Also, the cod balls can be baked up to 2 days in advance and refrigerated, tightly covered. Reheat them in a 350°F oven, uncovered, for 10 to 12 minutes, or until hot.

Variation:

✳ Substitute salmon or any firm-fleshed white fish like halibut or catfish for the cod.

> When a recipe calls for half a package of a frozen vegetable, allow the vegetable to thaw about halfway. Then slice through the package with a serrated knife, and then cover and return the remainder to the freezer.

New England Cod Balls

While living on Nantucket I devised myriad recipes to use the surrounding ocean's famed cod, and this is one of them. The crunchy potato chips add texture. These can also be made into large patties for sandwiches.

Makes 4 to 6 servings | *Active time: 20 minutes* | *Start to finish: 35 minutes*

2 tablespoons unsalted butter

1 small onion, finely chopped

½ green bell pepper, seeds and ribs removed, and finely chopped

1 large egg

1 cup Tartar Sauce (page 35) or purchased tartar sauce, divided

¾ cup finely crushed potato chips

2 tablespoons chopped fresh parsley

2 teaspoons fresh thyme or ½ teaspoon dried

Salt and freshly ground black pepper to taste

1¼ pounds cooked cod fillet, flaked

Vegetable oil spray

1. Preheat the oven to 425°F. Line a rimmed baking sheet with heavy-duty aluminum foil, and spray the foil with vegetable oil spray.

2. Heat butter in a small skillet over medium-high heat. Add onion and bell pepper, and cook, stirring frequently, for 3 to 5 minutes, or until onion is translucent. Set aside.

3. Combine egg and 2 tablespoons Tartar Sauce in a mixing bowl, and whisk well. Stir in crush potato chips, parsley, thyme, salt, and pepper, and then gently fold in cod.

4. Make mixture into 1½-inch balls, and arrange cod balls on the prepared pan. Spray tops of cod balls with vegetable oil spray. Bake cod balls for 12 to 15 minutes, or until cooked through. Remove the pan from the oven, and serve immediately, accompanied by a bowl of remaining Tartar Sauce for dipping.

Note: The cod mixture can be prepared up to 1 day in advance and refrigerated, tightly covered. Also, the cod balls can be baked up to 2 days in advance and refrigerated, tightly covered. Reheat them in a 350°F oven, uncovered, for 8 to 10 minutes, or until hot.

Variations:

* In addition to cooked fish or seafood of any kind, try cooked and finely chopped chicken or pork.

* Substitute 3 (6-ounce) cans of tuna fish, drained and flaked.

Cod are so important to New England's history that Cape Cod became the official name for the Massachusetts sandbar that juts out into the Atlantic Ocean. Cod are omnivorous, bottom-dwelling fish that are caught both in Nantucket Sound and in offshore waters. Scrod is a fancier term for small cod, since the fillets are thinner and can be sautéed easier than those taken from larger fish. In some restaurants, scrod can also be haddock; the two are similar in taste and texture.

Dill and Mustard Salmon Balls

The use of aromatic fresh dill is part of many diverse cuisines; they range from Greek to all of the Scandinavian countries. This dish has northern European inspiration because it blends the fresh herb with sharp mustard for a contrast.

Makes 4 to 6 servings | Active time: 25 minutes | Start to finish: 1¼ hours, including 30 minutes to chill mixture

1¼ pounds skinned salmon fillet

1 large egg

½ cup mayonnaise, divided

⅓ cup Dijon mustard, divided

1 cup plain breadcrumbs

⅓ cup chopped fresh dill, divided

Salt and freshly ground black pepper to taste

¼ cup sour cream

2 teaspoons freshly squeezed lemon juice

Vegetable oil spray

1. Rinse salmon, pat dry with paper towels, and cut into 1-inch pieces. Place salmon cubes on a sheet of plastic wrap, and freeze for 20 to 30 minutes, or until firm but not frozen solid.

2. Preheat the oven to 425°F. Line a rimmed baking sheet with heavy-duty aluminum foil, and spray the foil with vegetable oil spray.

3. Whisk egg, 2 tablespoons mayonnaise, and 2 tablespoons mustard in a mixing bowl, add ½ cup breadcrumbs and 3 tablespoons dill, and mix well. Chop salmon in a food processor using on-and-off pulsing.

Add salmon, season to taste with salt and pepper, and mix well again.

4. Make mixture into 1½-inch balls. Put remaining ½ cup breadcrumbs in a shallow bowl, and gently roll the balls in the crumbs. Arrange salmon balls on the prepared pan. Spray tops of salmon balls with vegetable oil spray.

5. Bake salmon balls for 12 to 15 minutes, or until cooked through. While salmon balls bake, combine remaining mayonnaise, sour cream, remaining mustard, remaining dill, and lemon juice in a mixing bowl, and whisk well. Remove the pan from the oven, and serve immediately, accompanied by the bowl of sauce for dipping.

Note: The salmon mixture can be prepared up to 1 day in advance and refrigerated, tightly covered. Also, the salmon balls can be baked up to 2 days in advance and refrigerated, tightly covered. Reheat them in a 350°F oven, uncovered, for 10 to 12 minutes, or until hot.

Variation:

∗ Substitute tuna or any firm-fleshed white fish like halibut or cod for the salmon.

A vegetable peeler and a pair of tweezers are the best ways to get rid of those pesky little bones in fish fillets. Run a peeler down the center of the fillet, starting at the tail end. It will catch the larger pin bones, and with a twist of your wrist, you can pull them out. For finer bones, use your fingers to rub the flesh lightly and then pull out the bones with the tweezers.

Chapter 9

Vibrant and Vegetarian:
Meatballs with Vegetables, Herbs, Legumes, and Grains

*A*ll of these recipes are for "meatballs" that contain no meat. Instead you'll find a wide range of foods bound together before being baked or fried. Many of them—such as dried beans—are an excellent source of protein and other nutrients too.

These recipes are all vegetarian, but most are not vegan because they include eggs and—frequently—cheese as well. A few uncooked cheese balls are included, too. In my carnivore household most of the recipes in this chapter are served as hors d'oeuvres or a side dish to elevate a simple entree to elegance. But many are satisfying enough to be served as a light lunch with a tossed salad. I include variations to make these vegetarian dishes into non-vegetarian ones. Serving sizes are main dish portions to remain consistent with recipes in the rest of the book. If serving them as a side dish, they can easily feed twice that number.

You may wonder why so many recipes in this chapter require frying. Since vegetables don't have a high protein content like meats, poultry, and fish, the ground up vegetable mixtures won't hold together when baked.

Falafel

Falafel are the potato chips of the Middle East, and they're as popular in Israel as in Arab countries. While they can be made with fava beans they are usually prepared with garbanzo beans, or chickpeas. What differentiates falafel from other bean balls is that the chickpeas are soaked— but not cooked— before they are ground into the paste. That is why dried beans are specified; canned beans would add too much moisture to the dish.

Makes 6 to 8 servings | *Active time: 30 minutes* | *Start to finish: 2½ hours, 1½ to soak beans*

1 pound dried garbanzo beans

1 small onion, diced

3 garlic cloves, peeled

4 tablespoons all-purpose flour

2 tablespoons chopped fresh parsley

1 tablespoon freshly squeezed lemon juice

1 tablespoon ground coriander

2 teaspoons ground cumin

1 teaspoon baking soda

Salt and cayenne to taste

3 cups vegetable oil for frying

FOR DIPPING:

1 cup Tahini (page 27)
or Middle Eastern Yogurt Sauce (page 33)

1. Soak garbanzo beans in cold water to cover for a minimum of 6 hours, or preferably overnight. Or, place beans in a saucepan covered with water, and bring to a boil over high heat. Boil for 1 minute, turn off the heat, and cover the pan. Allow beans to soak for 1 hour, then drain. With either method, continue with the dish as soon as beans have soaked, or refrigerate beans.

2. Drain beans and place them in the work bowl of a food processor. Add onion, garlic, flour, parsley, lemon juice, coriander, cumin, baking soda, salt, and cayenne. Process until the mixture forms a smooth paste, scraping the sides of the work bowl as necessary.

3. Form mixture into 1-inch balls, and refrigerate for 20 minutes, tightly covered with plastic wrap. Heat oil in a saucepan over medium-high heat to a temperature of 375°F.

4. Add falafel balls, being careful not to crowd the pan. Cook falafel balls for 3 minutes, or until browned. Remove falafel balls from the pan with a slotted spoon, and drain well on paper towels. Serve immediately, accompanied by a bowl of Tahini for dipping.

Note: The falafel balls can be prepared for frying up to 1 day in advance and refrigerated, tightly covered. They can also be fried in advance; reheat them in a 400°F oven for 5 to 7 minutes or until hot and crusty again.

Variation:

* Omit the coriander and cumin, and add 2 tablespoons chili powder; substitute cilantro for the parsley. This will make these more American than Middle Eastern.

Garbanzo beans, also called *chickpeas* and *ceci* in Italian, are legumes adored around the world for their nutlike flavor. Native to the Mediterranean, they found their way into dishes from India to Spain, with a lot of Middle Eastern cuisines included in the repertoire.

Italian Rice Balls

Arancini means "little oranges" in Italian, and these cheese-stuffed rice balls are a staple of Sicilian cooking. They go together quickly if you have some leftover risotto, so be sure to make some extra.

Makes 4 to 6 servings | Active time: 45 minutes | Start to finish: 3 hours, including 2 hours to chill mixture

RISOTTO:

3 tablespoons unsalted butter

1 medium onion, chopped

2 garlic cloves, minced

2 cups arborio rice

¾ cup white wine

5 cups chicken stock, heated to just below simmer

¾ cup freshly grated Parmesan

Salt and freshly ground black pepper to taste

RICE BALLS:

2 large eggs

2 cups risotto, chilled

½ cup freshly grated Parmesan

1½ cups seasoned Italian breadcrumbs, divided

2 ounces whole milk mozzarella, cut into ½-inch cubes

3 cups vegetable oil for frying

1. For risotto, place butter in a heavy saucepan over medium-high heat. Add onion and garlic, and cook, stirring frequently, for 3 minutes, or until onion is translucent. Add rice, and stir to coat with butter.

2. Raise the heat to high, add wine, and cook for 2 minutes, stirring constantly.

Reduce the heat to medium, and ladle 1 cup hot stock over rice. Stir constantly and wait for rice to absorb stock before adding next 1 cup, while stirring constantly. Repeat with stock until all 5 cups have been absorbed; this should take 12 to 15 minutes.

3. Stir cheese into rice, and season to taste with salt and pepper. Scrape rice into a 9x13-inch pan, and chill for at least 2 hours.

4. For rice balls, whisk eggs in a mixing bowl, and stir in risotto, cheese, and ½ cup breadcrumbs. Place remaining 1 cup breadcrumbs in a shallow bowl.

5. Measure out 1 tablespoon of rice mixture into your hand, and press a mozzarella cube into it. Top with another 1 tablespoon of rice mixture, and form into a ball; be careful to totally enclose cheese cube. Roll balls in breadcrumbs, and repeat until all of rice mixture is used.

6. Heat oil in a deep-sided saucepan or deep-fryer to a temperature of 375°F. Preheat the oven to 150°F, and line a baking sheet with paper towels.

7. Add rice balls, being careful not to crowd the pan. Cook rice balls for 3 to 4 minutes, or until browned. Remove rice balls from the pan with a slotted spoon, and drain well on paper towel-lined baking sheet. Keep fried rice balls warm in the oven while frying remaining balls. Serve immediately.

Note: The rice balls can be prepared for frying up to 1 day in advance and refrigerated, tightly covered. They can also be fried in advance; reheat them in a 400°F oven for 5 to 7 minutes or until hot and crusty again.

Variations:

✳ Add ½ teaspoon crushed saffron to the stock, and the rice balls will take on a bright yellow color.

✳ Cook ⅓ pound chopped wild mushrooms in 2 tablespoons unsalted butter and add them to the risotto as it cooks.

✳ Add 2 cups chopped fresh spinach or ½ of a 10-ounce package of frozen chopped spinach to the risotto as it cooks.

✳ Stir 1 cup pureed cooked asparagus into the stock while making the risotto.

Rice and Cheddar Balls

These fried morsels are an Americanized version of Sicilian *arancini*. Much of their flavor comes from the liquid in which the rice is cooked.

Makes 4 to 6 servings | *Active time: 30 minutes* | *Start to finish: 3½ hours, including 3 hours to chill mixture*

1 cup whole milk

1 cup long-grain white rice

2 tablespoons paprika

1 teaspoon dry mustard

2 tablespoons unsalted butter

4 scallions, white parts and 2-inches of green tops, chopped

½ red bell pepper, seeds and ribs removed, and finely chopped

2 large eggs

2 teaspoons fresh thyme or ½ teaspoon dried

2 cups grated cheddar cheese

Salt and freshly ground black pepper to taste

1 cup plain breadcrumbs

3 cups vegetable oil for frying

FOR DIPPING:

1 cup Herbed Tomato Sauce (page 21) or purchased marinara sauce, heated

1. Combine 1 cup water, milk, rice, paprika, and mustard in a saucepan, and stir well. Bring to a boil over medium-high heat, stirring occasionally. Cover the pan, reduce the heat to low, and cook for 15 to 18 minutes, or until liquid is absorbed and rice is tender. Remove the pan from the heat, and set aside.

2. While rice cooks, heat butter in a small skillet over medium-high heat. Add scallions and red pepper and cook, stirring frequently, for 5 minutes, or until vegetables soften.

3. Whisk eggs and thyme in a mixing bowl, and stir in rice, vegetable mixture, and cheese. Season to taste with salt and pepper, and mix well. Scrape mixture into a 9x13-inch pan, and refrigerate for at least 1 hour, or until well chilled.

4. Place breadcrumbs in a shallow bowl. Make mixture into 1½-inch balls, roll balls in breadcrumbs, and repeat until all of rice mixture is used.

5. Heat oil in a deep-sided saucepan or deep-fryer to a temperature of 375°F. Preheat the oven to 150°F, and line a baking sheet with paper towels.

6. Add rice balls, being careful not to crowd the pan. Cook rice balls for 3 to 4 minutes, or until browned. Remove balls from the pan with a slotted spoon, and drain well on paper towel-lined baking sheet. Keep fried rice balls warm in the oven while frying remaining balls.

Serve immediately, accompanied by a bowl of Herbed Tomato Sauce for dipping.

Note: The rice balls can be prepared for frying up to 1 day in advance and refrigerated, tightly covered. They can also be fried in advance; reheat them in a 400°F oven for 5 to 7 minutes, or until hot and crusty again.

Variations:

✳ Substitute Swiss or Gruyère for the cheddar.

✳ Omit the paprika and mustard, add 2 tablespoons the chili powder, and substitute jalapeño Jack for the cheddar.

✳ Omit the red bell pepper, and add ½ cup frozen chopped spinach, thawed and squeezed dry.

Corn Fritters

Crispy corn fritters are a wonderful hors d'oeuvre or side dish, and they are as at home on the breakfast table as the dinner table. The cornmeal in the recipe adds even more corn flavor.

Makes 4 to 6 servings | *Active time: 25 minutes* | *Start to finish: 25 minutes*

1 pound whole corn kernels (either cut fresh from the cob or frozen and thawed; do not use canned corn)

2 large eggs

3 scallions, white parts only, chopped

1 garlic clove, minced

3 tablespoons chopped fresh cilantro

1 cup all-purpose flour

¼ cup yellow cornmeal

1 tablespoon granulated sugar

3 teaspoons baking powder

2 teaspoons ground coriander

Salt and freshly ground black pepper to taste

3 cups vegetable oil for frying

FOR DIPPING:

1 cup Southern Barbecue Sauce (page 23) or purchased barbecue sauced, heated

1. Place corn in a saucepan, and cover with salted water. Bring to a boil over high heat, and cook for 2 minutes. Drain, and place corn in a blender or in a food processor. Add eggs, and puree until smooth. Scrape mixture into a mixing bowl.

2. Stir scallions, garlic, and cilantro into corn. Combine flour, cornmeal, sugar, baking powder, coriander, salt, and pepper in another mixing bowl, and whisk well. Stir dry ingredients into corn mixture, stirring until just combined.

3. Heat oil in a deep-sided saucepan or deep-fryer to a temperature of 375°F. Preheat the oven to 150°F, and line a baking sheet with paper towels.

4. Using a rubber spatula push batter off carefully into hot fat, about 1 tablespoonful at a time. Fry fritters until they are a deep golden brown, turning them in the hot fat to brown both sides. Remove fritters from the pan with a slotted spoon, and drain on paper towel-lined baking sheet. Keep fritters warm in the oven while frying remaining batter. Serve immediately, accompanied by a bowl of Southern Barbecue Sauce for dipping.

Note: The fritters can be prepared up to 2 days in advance and refrigerated, tightly covered. Reheat in a 375°F oven for 5 to 7 minutes, or until hot and crispy.

Variations:

* Omit the scallions, garlic, cilantro, and coriander; add an additional 1 tablespoon granulated sugar. Serve them for breakfast with heated pure maple syrup.

* Omit the cilantro and coriander, and add ¼ cup chopped pimiento and 1 teaspoon dried sage.

Baking powder does not last forever. If you haven't used it in a while try this test: Mix 2 teaspoons of baking powder with 1 cup of hot tap water. If there's an immediate reaction of fizzing and foaming, the baking powder can be used. If the reaction is delayed or weak, throw the baking powder away and buy a fresh can.

German Sauerkraut Balls

Anyone who grew up in the Midwest knows about sauerkraut balls; they are an integral part of many parties and spring from the German tradition. Mashed potatoes hold them together.

Makes 4 to 6 servings | *Active time: 30 minutes* | *Start to finish: 30 minutes*

1 pound potatoes, peeled

1 pound sauerkraut, drained well

2 large eggs

¾ cup grainy Dijon mustard, divided

3 scallions, white parts and 2 inches of green tops, chopped

2 tablespoons chopped fresh parsley

1 tablespoon crushed caraway seeds

Salt and freshly ground black pepper to taste

1 cup plain breadcrumbs

3 cups vegetable oil for frying

½ cup mayonnaise

½ cup sour cream

1. Dice potatoes into 1-inch cubes, and boil in salted water for 10 to 15 minutes, or until very tender. Drain potatoes, shaking in a colander to get out as much water as possible. Mash potatoes until smooth, and set aside.

2. While potatoes boil, soak sauerkraut in cold water, changing the water every 3 minutes. Drain sauerkraut, pressing with the back of a spoon to extract as much liquid as possible, and coarsely chop sauerkraut.

3. Whisk eggs and ¼ cup mustard in a mixing bowl, and add potatoes, sauerkraut, scallions, parsley, and caraway seeds. Mix well, and season to taste with salt and pepper.

4. Place breadcrumbs in a shallow bowl. Make mixture into 1½-inch balls, roll balls in breadcrumbs, and repeat until all of sauerkraut mixture is used.

5. Heat oil in a deep-sided saucepan to a temperature of 375°F. Preheat the oven to 150°F, and line a baking sheet with paper towels.

6. While oil heats, mix remaining ½ cup mustard with mayonnaise and sour cream, and whisk well. Set aside.

7. Add sauerkraut balls, being careful not to crowd the pan. Cook sauerkraut balls for 3 to 4 minutes, or until browned. Remove balls from the pan with a slotted spoon, and drain well on paper towel-lined baking sheet. Keep fried sauerkraut balls warm in the oven while frying remaining balls. Serve immediately, accompanied by the bowl of sauce for dipping.

Note: The sauerkraut balls can be prepared for frying up to 1 day in advance and refrigerated, tightly covered. They can also be fried in advance; reheat them in a 400°F oven for 5 to 7 minutes or until hot and crusty again.

Variations:

✳ Add 1 cup chopped ham or cooked sausage, such as smoked kielbasa.

✳ Add ½ cup grated cheese, such as cheddar or smoked cheddar.

> It's best to crush large seeds like caraway and fennel before adding them to a dish. The seeds release more flavor crushed, and they can be bitter if eaten whole. The easiest way to crush the seeds is with a mortar and pestle. If you don't have a mortar and pestle, place the seeds into a small, heavy plastic bag and pound them with the back of a small skillet or saucepan. This does the trick.

Cheese-Spinach Balls

These baked balls are a classic hors d'oeuvre. Serve them with Blue Cheese Sauce.

Makes 4 to 6 servings | Active time: 25 minutes | Start to finish: 40 minutes

1 (10-ounce) package frozen chopped spinach, thawed

6 tablespoons (¾ stick) unsalted butter

1 medium onion, chopped

2 garlic cloves, minced

3 large eggs

¾ cup freshly grated Parmesan

2 tablespoons chopped fresh parsley

1 tablespoon fresh thyme
or 1 teaspoon dried

1 cup seasoned Italian breadcrumbs, divided

Salt and freshly ground black pepper to taste

Vegetable oil spray

FOR DIPPING:

1 cup Blue Cheese Sauce (page 29) or purchased blue cheese dressing

1. Preheat the oven to 425°F. Line a rimmed baking sheet with heavy-duty aluminum foil, and spray the foil with vegetable oil spray. Place spinach in a colander and press with the back of a spoon to extract as much liquid as possible. Set aside.

2. Heat butter in a small skillet over medium-high heat. Add onion and garlic and cook, stirring frequently, for 3 minutes, or until onion is translucent. Set aside.

3. Whisk eggs well, and stir in spinach, onion mixture, cheese, parsley, thyme, ½ cup breadcrumbs, salt, and pepper. Mix well.

4. Place remaining ½ cup breadcrumbs in a shallow bowl, make mixture into 1½-inch balls, roll balls in breadcrumbs, and arrange spinach balls on the prepared pan. Spray tops of spinach balls with vegetable oil spray.

5. Bake spinach balls for 12 to 15 minutes, or until cooked through. Remove the pan from the oven, and serve immediately, accompanied by a bowl of Blue Cheese Sauce for dipping.

Note: The spinach mixture can be prepared up to 1 day in advance and refrigerated, tightly covered. Also, the balls can be baked up to 2 days in advance and refrigerated, tightly covered. Reheat them in a 350°F oven, covered, for 10 to 12 minutes, or until hot.

Variations:

* Replace the spinach with finely chopped broccoli or asparagus.
* Make these balls with cheddar instead of Parmesan.

The best place to store eggs is in their cardboard carton. The carton helps prevent moisture loss, and it shields the eggs from absorbing odors from other foods. If you're not sure if your eggs are fresh, submerge them in a bowl of cool water. If they stay on the bottom, they're fine. If they float to the top, it shows they're old because eggs develop an air pocket at one end as they age.

Italian Eggplant Balls

In Southern Italy meat was quite scarce, so cooks invented dishes using eggplant and other vegetables. *Pitticelle di murignani* come from Calabria, the point of Italy's boot.

Makes 4 to 6 servings | Active time: 30 minutes | Start to finish: 1½ hours

3 (1-pound) eggplants

2 large eggs

½ cup freshly grated Parmesan

1½ cups seasoned Italian breadcrumbs, divided

3 tablespoons chopped fresh parsley

2 tablespoons chopped fresh oregano or 2 teaspoons dried

Salt and freshly ground black pepper to taste

3 cups vegetable oil for frying

FOR DIPPING:

1 cup Herbed Tomato Sauce (page 21) or purchased marinara sauce, heated

1. Preheat the oven to 450°F, and line a rimmed baking sheet with heavy-duty aluminum foil. Prick eggplants with a meat fork, and bake for 20 minutes. Turn eggplants over and bake for an additional 20 minutes, or until eggplants are totally tender. Remove the pan from the oven, and cut eggplants in half. When cool enough to handle, scrape pulp away from skin, and puree in a food processor, adding juices that have accumulated in the pan. Scrape eggplant into a mixing bowl.

2. Whisk eggs in a mixing bowl, and add eggplant puree, cheese, ½ cup breadcrumbs, parsley, oregano, salt, and pepper. Add more breadcrumbs, if necessary, to form a cohesive dough.

3. Place remaining 1 cup breadcrumbs in a shallow bowl. Make mixture into 1½-inch balls, roll balls in breadcrumbs, and repeat until all of eggplant mixture is used.

4. Heat oil in a deep-sided saucepan or deep-fryer to a temperature of 375°F. Preheat the oven to 150°F, and line a baking sheet with paper towels.

5. Add eggplant balls, being careful not to crowd the pan. Cook eggplant balls for 3 to 4 minutes, or until browned. Remove eggplant balls from the pan with a slotted spoon, and drain well on paper towel-lined baking sheet. Keep fried eggplant balls warm in the oven while frying remaining balls. Serve immediately, accompanied by a bowl of Herbed Tomato Sauce for dipping.

Note: The eggplant balls can be prepared for frying up to 1 day in advance and refrigerated, tightly covered. They can also be fried in advance; reheat them in a 400°F oven for 5 to 7 minutes, or until hot and crusty again.

Variations:

＊ For Sicilian eggplant balls, add ½ cup toasted pine nuts and ½ cup dried currants (soaked in hot water for 10 minutes and then drained) to the eggplant mixture.

＊ For Neapolitan eggplant balls, add ½ cup chopped pitted green or black olives to the eggplant mixture.

Eggplants have male and female gender, and the males are preferable since they have fewer seeds. Choose a male eggplant since it is less bitter and has less seeds. To tell a male from a female, look at the stem end. The male is rounded and has a more even hole, and the female hole is indented.

Chapter 10

Meatballs in Broth:

Main Course Soups

There's an old Spanish proverb: "Of soup and love, the first is best."
A bowl of steaming soup says "comfort food" on a cold winter's night, and homey meatballs are a welcome addition that can turn a starter into an entire meal. Hearty soups exist in every culture, and you'll find a wide range of recipes in this chapter. The meatballs included in the soups are all made small so that they fit on your soupspoon without cutting.

We start out with recipes for beef and chicken stocks. Stocks are the "secret weapon" of why soups and sauces served in fine restaurants are frequently superior to those made at home with canned stocks. If you get into the habit of "stocking up" you will find that while you are gaining nutrients and flavor, you're also saving money. Think about those limp carrots and onion peels destined for the trash. Instead, they can be in your freezer and joined by some chicken bones, and for pennies you can make a few quarts of stock.

So think about these hearty, healthful soups as a meal in a bowl, and enjoy all the emotional satisfaction that goes along with preparing—and eating them.

Beef Stock

Browning the meat adds a rich brown color and slightly caramelized flavor to this stock, which is the backbone of so many meat-based recipes. When cutting up a chuck roast to make stew, or trimming fat off of beef before broiling it, save those scraps to add to your stock.

Makes 2 quarts | Active time: 15 minutes | Start to finish: 3½ hours

2 pounds beef shank (or 1 pound beef stew meat or chuck roast)

1 carrot, cut into thick slices

1 medium onion, sliced

1 celery rib, sliced

1 tablespoon whole black peppercorns

3 sprigs fresh parsley

3 sprigs fresh thyme or 1 teaspoon dried

2 garlic cloves, peeled

1 bay leaf

1. Preheat the oven broiler. Line a broiler pan with heavy-duty aluminum foil. Broil beef for 3 minutes per side, or until browned. Transfer beef to a large stockpot, and add 2 quarts water. Bring to a boil over high heat. Reduce the heat to low, and skim off foam that rises during the first 10 to 15 minutes of simmering. Simmer for 1 hour, uncovered, then add carrot, onion, celery, peppercorns, parsley, thyme, garlic, and bay leaf. Simmer for 3 hours.

2. Strain stock through a fine-meshed sieve, pushing with the back of a spoon to extract as much liquid as possible. Discard solids, divide stock among small plastic containers, and refrigerate. Before using, remove and discard fat from surface of stock.

Note: The stock can be refrigerated and used within 3 days, or it can be frozen up to 6 months.

Chicken Stock

Richly flavored, homemade chicken stock is as important as good olive oil in my kitchen, and it's as easy to make as boiling water. Keep a plastic bag in your freezer for the skin and other tidbits that are trimmed off chicken before it's cooked. When the bag is full, it's time to make stock.

Makes 3 quarts
Active time: 10 minutes | *Start to finish: 3½ hours*

5 pounds chicken bones, skin, and trimmings
4 celery ribs, cut into thick slices
2 onions, quartered
2 carrots, cut into thick slices
2 tablespoons whole black peppercorns
6 garlic cloves, peeled
4 sprigs parsley
4 sprigs thyme or 1 teaspoon dried
2 bay leaves

1. Place 6 quarts water and chicken in a large stockpot, and bring to a boil over high heat. Reduce the heat to low, and skim off foam that rises during the first 10 to 15 minutes of simmering. Simmer stock, uncovered, for 1 hour, then add celery, onions, carrots, peppercorns, garlic, parsley, thyme, and bay leaves. Simmer for 2½ hours.

2. Strain stock through a fine-meshed sieve, pushing with the back of a spoon to extract as much liquid as possible. Discard solids, divide stock among small plastic containers, and refrigerate. Remove and discard fat from surface of stock.

Note: The stock can be refrigerated and used within 3 days, or it can be frozen up to 6 months.

Quick Chicken Stock

Here's a way to make a reasonable facsimile of stock in just a few minutes.

Makes 2 quarts
Active time: 10 minutes | *Start to finish: 30 minutes*

2 quarts canned low-sodium chicken stock
4 celery ribs, finely chopped
1 onion, diced
2 carrots, finely chopped
2 tablespoons whole black peppercorns
6 garlic cloves, peeled
4 sprigs parsley
4 sprigs thyme or 1 teaspoon dried
2 bay leaves

1. Combine purchased stock, celery, onion, carrots, peppercorns, garlic, parsley, thyme, and bay leaves in a large stockpot, and bring to a boil over high heat. Reduce the heat to low, cover the pan, and simmer 20 minutes.

2. Strain stock through a fine-meshed sieve, pressing with the back of a spoon to extract as much liquid as possible. Divide stock into small plastic containers, and refrigerate when cool.

Note: The stock can be refrigerated and used within 3 days, or it can be frozen up to 6 months.

Chicken Vegetable Soup with Matzo Balls

Sometimes called "Jewish Penicillin," a hearty bowl of chicken soup with light and fluffy dumplings made from eggs and ground matzo wafers doesn't need an excuse like a cold to enjoy. You'll find matzo meal in the international food aisle of most supermarkets.

Makes 6 to 8 servings | *Active time: 15 minutes* | *Start to finish: 1½ hours, including 30 minutes for dough to chill*

MATZO BALLS:

4 large eggs

¼ cup chicken stock

¼ cup vegetable oil

1 cup matzo meal

Salt and freshly ground black pepper to taste

SOUP:

8 cups Chicken Stock (page 199) or purchased stock

2 carrots, sliced

1 small onion, diced

1 celery rib, sliced

½ cup fresh peas or frozen peas, thawed

½ cup diced fresh string beans or frozen beans, thawed

Salt and freshly ground black pepper to taste

1. For matzo balls, place eggs in a mixing bowl, and whisk well with stock and oil. Stir in matzo meal, and season to taste with salt and pepper. Refrigerate mixture for at least 30 minutes.

2. Bring a large pot of salted water to a boil. Using wet hands, form matzo dough into 1-inch balls, and drop them into water. Cover the pot, reduce the heat to low, and simmer matzo balls for 35 minutes *without removing the cover from the pan.*

3. While matzo balls simmer, heat stock to a boil over medium-high heat. Add carrots, celery, and onion, reduce the heat to low, and cook vegetables, uncovered, for 10 to 12 minutes, or until carrots are tender. Add peas and string beans, and cook for an additional 5 minutes.

4. Remove matzo balls from the pan with a slotted spoon, and transfer them to soup. Season to taste with salt and pepper, and serve immediately.

Note: The soup can be made up to 2 days in advance and refrigerated, tightly covered. Reheat it over low heat, covered.

Variations:

＊ Add ¾ cup frozen chopped spinach, thawed and squeezed dry.

＊ Add ¼ cup chopped fresh dill.

＊ Add 2 tablespoons chopped fresh parsley, 2 teaspoons fresh thyme, and 2 teaspoons chopped fresh sage.

＊ Add ½ pound fresh shiitake mushrooms, sautéed.

＊ Add 2 tablespoons of tomato paste.

Matzo, also spelled *matzah*, is the traditional unleavened bread eaten by Jews for the week they celebrate Passover each year. The holiday commemorates the Jews' flight from Egypt, at which time they no time for their bread to rise.

Spicy Thai Chicken Meatball Soup

Main course soups are part of every Asian cuisine, such as this one drawn from classic Thai cooking. The broth is laced with assertive flavors like ginger and chilies, and the delicate meatballs are cooked right in the soup.

Makes 4 to 6 servings | *Active time: 20 minutes* | *Start to finish: 40 minutes*

SOUP:

1 cup dried shiitake mushrooms

1 (1-ounce) package cellophane noodles

1 cup firmly packed fresh cilantro leaves

1 tablespoon grated fresh ginger

3 garlic cloves, minced

1 jalapeño or serrano chile, seeds and ribs removed, and chopped

2 tablespoons fish sauce (nam pla)

1 tablespoon firmly packed light brown sugar

7 cups Chicken Stock (page 199) or purchased stock

Salt and freshly ground black pepper to taste

MEATBALLS:

3 tablespoons fish sauce (nam pla)

3 tablespoons cornstarch

1¼ pounds ground chicken

3 garlic cloves, pushed through a garlic press

1 tablespoon Asian sesame oil

FOR GARNISH:

Sliced scallions

Fresh cilantro leaves

1. Combine shiitake mushrooms and 1 cup boiling water, pushing them down into the water. Soak for 10 minutes, then drain mushrooms, reserving soaking liquid. Discard stems, and chop mushrooms. Set aside. Strain soaking liquid through a sieve lined with a paper coffee filter or paper towel. While mushrooms soak, follow package directions and soak cellophane noodles. Drain, and cut into 2-inch lengths with sharp scissors.

2. While ingredients soak, make meatballs. Combine fish sauce and cornstarch in a mixing bowl, and stir well. Add chicken, garlic, and sesame oil, and mix well. Form mixture into ¾-inch balls, and set aside.

3. For soup, combine cilantro, ginger, garlic, chili, fish sauce, and brown sugar in a food processor fitted with a steel blade or in a blender. Puree until smooth. Scrape mixture into a 3-quart saucepan, and stir in chicken stock and reserved mushroom soaking liquid. Bring to a boil over medium-high heat, stirring occasionally.

4. Add meatballs, reduce the heat to low, and cook soup, uncovered, for 5 to 8 minutes, or until meatballs are cooked through and no longer pink. Add noodles and mushrooms, and simmer 2 minutes more. Season to taste with salt and pepper, ladle soup into bowls, and sprinkle each serving with scallions and cilantro.

Note: The soup can be made up to 2 days in advance and refrigerated, tightly covered. Reheat it over low heat, covered.

Variations:

✳ A combination of ground shrimp and cod for a lighter flavor.

✳ To add more protein, add 1 cup diced extra-firm tofu to the broth.

✳ Add sliced bok choy to the soup at the same time as the meatballs to increase the vegetable content without diluting the flavor.

Mexican Turkey Meatball Soup

Crushed corn tortilla chips not only add their earthy flavor to this soup, they also provide some crunch; unlike breadcrumbs, the tortilla chips retain their texture. This is my version of tortilla soup, and the cornucopia of vegetables makes it a meal.

Makes 4 to 6 servings | *Active time: 20 minutes* | *Start to finish: 45 minutes*

MEATBALLS:

1 large egg

¼ cup tomato juice

2 garlic cloves, minced

2 teaspoons ground cumin

1 teaspoon dried oregano

1¼ pounds ground turkey

½ cup crushed tortilla chips

Salt and freshly ground black pepper to taste

Vegetable oil spray

SOUP:

¼ cup olive oil

1 large onion, diced

2 garlic cloves, minced

1 cup seeded, diced green or red pepper (or ½ cup each)

2 tablespoons chili powder

6 cups Chicken Stock (page 199) or purchased stock

2 (14.5-ounce) cans petite diced tomatoes, undrained

2 celery ribs, sliced

2 carrots, sliced

1 (15-ounce) can kidney beans, drained and rinsed

1 cup fresh corn kernels or frozen kernels, thawed

½ cup fresh peas or frozen peas, thawed

1. Preheat the oven to 450°F. Cover a rimmed baking sheet with heavy-duty aluminum foil, and spray the foil with vegetable oil spray.

2. Combine egg, tomato juice, garlic, cumin, and oregano in medium mixing bowl, and whisk well. Add turkey and tortilla chips, season to taste with salt and pepper, and mix well. Make mixture into 1-inch meatballs, and arrange meatballs on the prepared pan. Spray tops of meatballs with vegetable oil spray. Bake meatballs for 12 to 15 minutes.

3. While meatballs bake, heat olive oil in heavy 3-quart saucepan over medium-high heat. Add onion and garlic, and cook, stirring frequently, for 2 minutes. Add chopped peppers and continue to saute for 2 more minutes or until onion is translucent. Stir in chili powder, and cook for 1 minute, stirring constantly. Stir in chicken stock, tomatoes, celery, and carrots.

4. Bring to a boil and simmer soup, uncovered, for 20 minutes, or until vegetables are tender. Add meatballs, kidney beans, corn, and peas to soup, and simmer for 5 minutes. Season to taste with salt and pepper, and serve immediately.

Note: The soup can be made up to 2 days in advance and refrigerated, tightly covered. Reheat it over low heat, covered.

Variations:

✳ Make the meatballs from beef or a combination of beef and pork.

✳ Use any sort of canned bean in your larder; there's no reason to purchase kidney beans if you have others around.

> Be careful when adding to salt to dishes that contain a salted food such as tortilla chips. Chances are the meatball mixture will need very little, if any, salt because the salt from the chips is part of the mixture.

Italian Wedding Soup with Turkey Meatballs

Wedding soup is actually an Italian-American creation, not a classic Italian dish. It is a mistranslation of *minestra maritata* which has nothing to do with nuptials, but is a reference to the fact that green vegetables and meats go well together. Tasty greens, swirls of egg, lots of heady Parmesan and flavorful meatballs are what you'll find in this easy to prepare soup. Serve it with a loaf of garlic bread and your meal is complete.

Makes 6 to 8 servings | *Active time: 20 minutes* | *Start to finish: 1 hour*

MEATBALLS:

1 large egg

½ cup seasoned Italian breadcrumbs

¼ cup whole milk

1 small onion, grated

2 garlic cloves, minced

¼ cup chopped fresh Italian parsley

½ cup freshly grated Parmesan

1½ pounds ground turkey

Salt and freshly ground black pepper to taste

SOUP:

8 cups Chicken Stock (page 199) or purchased stock

1 pound curly endive, rinsed, cored, and coarsely chopped

2 large eggs

½ cup freshly grated Parmesan, divided

Salt and freshly ground black pepper to taste

1. Combine egg, breadcrumbs, milk, onion, garlic, parsley, and Parmesan, and mix well. Add turkey, season to taste with salt and pepper, and mix well into a paste.

2. Combine chicken stock and endive in a 3-quart saucepan, and bring to a boil over medium-high heat. Reduce the heat to low, and simmer soup, uncovered, for 10 minutes.

3. Using wet hands, form meatball mixture into 1-inch balls, and drop them into simmering soup. Cook for 7 to 10 minutes, or until cooked through and no longer pink.

4. Whisk eggs with 2 tablespoons cheese. Stir soup and gradually add egg mixture to form thin strands. Season to taste with salt and pepper, and serve immediately, passing remaining cheese separately.

Note: The soup can be made up to 2 days in advance and refrigerated, tightly covered. Reheat it over low heat, covered.

Variations:

* Substitute escarole for the curly endive.
* Pork, or a combination of pork and veal, are equally delicious for the meatballs.

Parmesan cheese is one of the distinctive and delectable ingredients in Italian cooking. Its flavor and aroma, however, dissipate quickly once the cheese is grated. That's why it's worth the effort to grate the real thing—Parmigiano-Reggiano-- while cooking each recipe.

Onion Soup with Gruyère-Beef Meatballs

There's nothing like a steaming bowl of onion soup to warm your body on a winter night, and the addition of hearty meatballs made with Gruyère makes it a meal. The addition of red wine to the stock deepens the color of the soup as well as enhancing its flavor.

Makes 6 to 8 servings | *Active time: 25 minutes* | *Start to finish: 1¼ hours*

SOUP:

3 tablespoons unsalted butter

1 tablespoon olive oil

3 pounds yellow onions, thinly sliced

1 teaspoon granulated sugar

3 tablespoons all-purpose flour

2 quarts Beef Stock (page 197) or purchased stock

¾ cup dry red wine

3 tablespoons chopped fresh parsley

1 tablespoon fresh thyme or 1 teaspoon dried

1 bay leaf

Salt and freshly ground black pepper to taste

MEATBALLS:

3 slices white bread

2 tablespoons whole milk

2 tablespoons unsalted butter

1 small onion, finely chopped

2 garlic cloves, minced

1 large egg

1½ pounds ground chuck

2 tablespoons chopped fresh parsley

¾ cup grated Gruyère

Salt and freshly ground black pepper to taste

Vegetable oil spray

1. For soup, heat butter and oil in a large saucepan over low heat. Add onions, toss to coat with fat, and cover the pan. Cook over low heat for 10 minutes, stirring occasionally. Uncover the pan, raise the heat to medium, and stir in sugar. Cook for 30 to 40 minutes, stirring frequently, until onions are dark brown.

2. Reduce the heat to low, stir in flour, and cook for 2 minutes, stirring constantly. Stir in stock, wine, parsley, thyme, and bay leaf. Bring soup to a boil and simmer, partially covered, for 40 minutes. Season to taste with salt and pepper; remove and discard bay leaf.

3. While soup simmers, prepare meatballs. Preheat the oven to 450°F. Line a rimmed baking sheet with heavy-duty aluminum foil, and spray the foil with vegetable oil spray. Tear bread into small pieces, and place in a bowl with milk; stir well.

4. Heat butter in a small skillet over medium-high heat. Add onion and garlic, and cook, stirring frequently, for 3 minutes, or until onion is translucent. While vegetables cook, whisk egg in a mixing bowl, and add bread mixture, beef, parsley, and cheese.

5. Add onion mixture to the mixing bowl, season to taste with salt and pepper, and mix well. Make mixture into 1-inch meatballs, and arrange meatballs on the prepared pan. Spray tops of meatballs with vegetable oil spray.

6. Bake meatballs for 8 to 10 minutes, or until cooked through. Remove the pan from the oven, and set aside. Add meatballs to soup, season to taste with salt and pepper, and serve immediately.

Note: The soup can be made up to 2 days in advance and refrigerated, tightly covered. Reheat it over low heat, covered.

Variations:
* Although not classicly French, red onions impart a sweeter flavor.
* Instead of Gruyère, try Italian provolone or cheddar in the meatballs.

Chinese Hot and Sour Soup with Pork Meatballs

Unlike many dishes found on Chinese restaurant menus in North America, hot and sour soup is authentically Chinese; it comes from Szechwan province. The thick and hearty broth and flavorful meatballs are joined by healthful tofu in this satisfying dish.

Makes 4 to 6 servings | *Active time: 20 minutes* | *Start to finish: 40 minutes*

MEATBALLS:

½ cup dried shiitake mushrooms

1 cup boiling water

1 large egg

2 tablespoons soy sauce

4 scallions, white parts and 3-inches of green tops, chopped

2 garlic cloves, minced

1¼ pounds ground pork

1 cup cooked white rice

Freshly ground black pepper to taste

Vegetable oil spray

SOUP:

2 tablespoons vegetable oil

2 tablespoons Asian sesame oil

6 scallions, white parts and 3-inches of green tops, sliced

3 garlic cloves, minced

6 cups Chicken Stock (page 199) or purchased

⅓ cup rice wine vinegar

¼ cup soy sauce

2 tablespoons dry sherry

½ to 1 teaspoon freshly ground black pepper

½ pound firm tofu, drained, rinsed, and cut into ½-inch cubes

2 tablespoons cornstarch

3 large eggs, lightly beaten

Salt and freshly ground black pepper to taste

1. Preheat the oven to 450°F. Line a rimmed baking sheet with heavy-duty aluminum foil, and spray the foil with vegetable oil spray.

2. Combine shiitake mushrooms and boiling water, pushing them down into the water. Soak for 10 minutes, then drain mushrooms, reserving soaking liquid. Discard stems, and chop mushrooms. Strain liquid through a sieve lined with a paper coffee filter or paper towel. Set aside.

3. Combine eggs, soy sauce, scallion, and garlic, and whisk well. Add pork, rice, and mushrooms, season to taste with salt, and mix well. Make mixture into 1-inch meatballs, and arrange meatballs on the prepared pan. Spray tops of meatballs with vegetable oil spray.

4. Bake meatballs for 8 to 10 minutes, or until well browned. Remove the pan from the oven, and set aside.

5. While meatballs bake, heat vegetable oil and sesame oil in a heavy 3-quart saucepan over medium-high heat. Add scallions and garlic and cook, stirring frequently, for 1 minute. Stir in chicken stock, rice vinegar, soy sauce, sherry, reserved mushroom soaking liquid, and pepper. Bring to a boil, and simmer soup, uncovered, for 10 minutes. Add tofu and meatballs, and simmer for an additional 10 minutes.

6. Combine cornstarch and 2 tablespoons cold water in a small bowl. Add to soup, and simmer for 2 minutes, or until lightly thickened. Slowly add egg while stirring. Simmer 1 minute, season to taste with salt and pepper, and serve immediately.

Note: The soup can be made up to 2 days in advance and refrigerated, tightly covered. Reheat it over low heat, covered.

Variations:

✻ Make the balls from shrimp or a combination of shrimp and pork.

✻ Add some fresh shiitake mushrooms or dried shiitake which have been rehydrated to the broth.

New England Chowder with Clam Fritters

Early chowder recipes call for everything from beer to ketchup, but not milk. What we know as New England chowder dates from the mid-nineteenth century.

Makes 4 to 6 servings | *Active time: 25 minutes* | *Start to finish: 50 minutes*

SOUP:

1 pint fresh chopped clams

4 tablespoons (½ stick) unsalted butter, divided

2 medium onions, diced

2 celery ribs, sliced

1 (8-ounce) bottle clam juice

2 medium red potatoes, cut into ½-inch dice

2 tablespoons chopped fresh parsley

1 bay leaf

1 tablespoon fresh thyme or 1 teaspoon dried

3 tablespoons all-purpose flour

2 cups whole milk

1 cup heavy cream or half-and-half

Salt and freshly ground black pepper to taste

FRITTERS:

1 large egg

¾ cup whole milk

1½ cups all-purpose flour

1½ teaspoons baking powder

Clams reserved from the soup recipe

2 scallions, white parts only, finely chopped

Salt and freshly ground black pepper to taste

3 cups vegetable oil for frying

1. For soup, drain clams in a sieve over a bowl, reserving juice in the bowl. Press down with the back of a spoon to extract as much liquid as possible from clams. Refrigerate clams until ready to use.

2. Melt 2 tablespoons butter in a large saucepan over medium heat. Add onions and celery, and cook, stirring frequently, for 3 minutes, or until onions are translucent. Add bottled clam juice and reserved clam juice to the pan, along with potatoes, parsley, bay leaf, and thyme. Bring to a boil, reduce the heat to low, and simmer, covered, for 12 minutes, or until potatoes are tender.

3. While mixture simmers, melt remaining 2 tablespoons butter in a small saucepan over low heat. Stir in flour and cook, stirring constantly, for 2 minutes. Raise the heat to medium and whisk in milk. Bring to a boil, whisking frequently, and simmer for 2 minutes. Stir thickened milk into the pot with vegetables, and add cream.

Bring to a boil, reduce the heat to low, and simmer, uncovered, for 3 minutes. Remove and discard bay leaf, season to taste with salt and pepper, and keep hot.

4. While vegetables simmer, make clam fritters. Combine egg and milk in a mixing bowl, and whisk well. Add flour and baking powder, and whisk well. Stir in reserved clams and scallions, and season to taste with salt and pepper.

5. Preheat the oven to 150°F. Line a baking sheet with paper towels. Heat oil in a deep-sided saucepan over medium-high heat to a temperature of 375°F. Drop fritter batter by 1-tablespoon amounts into hot oil, and fry for 2 to 3 minutes, or until golden brown, turning as necessary with a slotted spoon. Remove fritters, and drain on paper towel-lined baking sheet. Place fritters in the oven, and repeat until all batter is fried.

6. To serve, ladle soups into bowls, and top each serving with fritters.

Chapter 11

Bonus Round:

Desserts

This chapter stretches the definition of "meatball" to new meanings, but there are so many wonderful sweet things that are "ground and round" that it make sense to end this book on a sweet note.

These quick and easy-to-make recipes range include homemade chocolate truffles, baby cream puffs filled with ice cream, baked and unbaked cookies, and some sweet fritters, which are bits of fried batter to be enjoyed hot. While many of these recipes are distinctly American, some come from cuisines around the world.

The key to the success in the recipes that use chocolate is to buy high-quality chocolate since it plays a starring role. While I like imported chocolate sold in big hunks, there are many excellent domestic brands now available. Look for a chocolate that contains at least 60 percent cocoa.

Chocolate Truffles

Once you learn how easy it is to make these truffles, you'll never buy those expensive one again. See the many variations for making truffles in your favorite flavors—from mint to orange to espresso.

Makes 3 dozen | Active time: 20 minutes | Start to finish: 4½ hours, including 4 hours to chill

1 pound good-quality bittersweet chocolate
1¼ cups heavy cream
Pinch of salt
½ cup unsweetened cocoa powder

1. Break chocolate into pieces no larger than a lima bean. Either chop chocolate in a food processor using on-and-off pulsing, or place it in a heavy resealable plastic bag, and smash it with the back of a heavy skillet.

2. Heat cream in a saucepan over medium heat, stirring frequently, until mixture comes to a simmer. Stir in salt, and add chocolate. Remove the pan from the heat, cover the pan, and allow chocolate to melt for 5 minutes. Whisk mixture until smooth, and transfer to a 9 x 9-inch baking pan. Chill mixture for at least 4 hours, or overnight.

3. Place cocoa powder in a shallow bowl. Using the large side of a melon baller, scoop out 2 teaspoons mixture, and gently form it into a ball. Roll balls in cocoa, and then refrigerate on a platter for 30 minutes to set cocoa.

Note: The truffles can be made up to 1 week in advance, and refrigerated, tightly covered with plastic wrap or in an airtight container. Allow them to sit at room temperature for 1 hour before serving.

Variations:
* Instead of cocoa powder, coat the truffles in toasted coconut, finely chopped nuts, or colored candy sprinkles.
* Add 2 to 4 tablespoons liquor or liqueur to the truffle mixture.
* Add 1 to 2 tablespoons instant coffee powder or instant espresso powder to make mocha truffles.
* Add 1 tablespoon grated orange zest to the mixture.
* Form truffles around a small nut, such as a hazelnut or a peanut.
* Coat truffles in dark chocolate or white chocolate or some combination of the two. To do this, melt chopped chocolate in a mixing bowl set over simmering water, or place chopped chocolate in a microwave safe bowl and microwave on 100% (HIGH) for 20 seconds, stir, and repeat as necessary until chocolate is smooth and melted. Place a small amount of melted chocolate in the palm of your hand, and roll formed balls in the chocolate.

> **Shaping the truffles easy is easier with cold hands. Keep a bowl of ice water and a roll of paper towels handy while rolling the truffles. Submerge your hands in the water until they are very cold. Then dry them and roll some truffles, repeating as necessary.**

Chocolate Goat Cheese Truffles

The sharpness of goat cheese balances the sweetness of the chocolate for these unusual confections.

Makes 4 dozen | *Active time: 30 minutes* | *Start to finish: 2 hours, including 1½ hours to chill*

½ pound good-quality bittersweet chocolate, chopped or shaved

½ pound fresh goat cheese

¼ cup confectioners' sugar

½ teaspoon pure vanilla extract

½ cup unsweetened cocoa powder

1. Break chocolate into pieces no larger than a lima bean. Either chop chocolate in a food processor using on-and-off pulsing, or place it in a heavy resealable plastic bag, and smash it with the back of a heavy skillet.

2. Melt chopped chocolate in a mixing bowl set over simmering water, or place chopped chocolate in a microwave safe bowl and microwave on 100% (HIGH) for 20 seconds, stir, and repeat as necessary until chocolate is smooth and melted.

3. Combine goat cheese, confectioners' sugar, and vanilla in a mixing bowl and beat at medium speed with an electric mixer until light and fluffy; this can also be done in a food processor. Slowly add chocolate, and beat until well mixed. Scrape mixture into a 9 x 9-inch baking pan, and refrigerate for at least 1 hour, or until firm.

4. Place cocoa powder in a shallow bowl. Using the large side of a melon baller, scoop out 2 teaspoons mixture, and gently form it into a ball. Roll balls in cocoa, and then refrigerate for 30 minutes to set cocoa.

Note: The truffles can be made up to 1 week in advance, and refrigerated, tightly covered with plastic wrap or in an airtight container. Allow them to sit at room temperature for 1 hour before serving.

Variations:
✽ Add 2 tablespoons of your favorite liqueur or liquor.
✽ Roll the balls in shaved white chocolate instead of cocoa.

Cocoa powder has a tendency to become lumpy when exposed to humidity, so sift the cocoa or shake it through a fine-meshed sieve before using it. Those little lumps are difficult to remove otherwise.

Extra-Chocolaty Truffles

These truffles are for those who like chocolate but not too much sugar in their confections. Adding unsweetened cocoa powder to the mix brings increases the intense chocolate flavor.

Makes 2½ dozen | Active time: 20 minutes | Start to finish: 4½ hours, including 4 hours to chill

½ pound good-quality bittersweet chocolate

½ cup heavy whipping cream

4 tablespoons (½ stick) unsalted butter, cut into small pieces

Pinch of salt

⅔ cup unsweetened cocoa powder, divided

1. Break chocolate into pieces no larger than a lima bean. Either chop chocolate in a food processor using on-and-off pulsing, or place it in a heavy resealable plastic bag, and smash it with the back of a heavy skillet.

2. Heat cream and butter in a saucepan over medium heat, stirring frequently, until mixture comes to a simmer. Stir in salt, and add chocolate and ¼ cup cocoa. Remove the pan from the heat, cover the pan, and allow chocolate to melt for 5 minutes. Whisk mixture until smooth, and transfer to a 9 x 9-inch baking pan. Chill mixture for at least 4 hours, or overnight.

3. Place remaining cocoa powder in a shallow bowl. Using the large side of a melon baller, scoop out 2 teaspoons mixture, and gently form it into a ball. Roll balls in cocoa, and then refrigerate for 30 minutes to set cocoa.

Note: The truffles can be made up to 1 week in advance, and refrigerated, tightly covered with plastic wrap or in an airtight container. Allow them to sit at room temperature for 1 hour before serving.

Variations:

✻ Use milk chocolate in place of bittersweet chocolate.

✻ Add ½ cup chopped toasted nuts to the mixture.

When cooking, use butter that comes in stick, not whipped butter sold in tubs. The air incorporated into whipped butter will throw off the recipe's measurements.

Booze-Laced Balls

These unbaked balls, popular at the holiday season for generations, are made crushed cookies and have some sort of spirit or liqueur added to them—in this case, bourbon.

Makes 5 dozen | Active time: 30 minutes | Start to finish: 4½ hours, including 4 hours to chill

1 cup pecan halves
1½ cups confectioners' sugar, divided
¼ cup unsweetened cocoa powder
½ cup bourbon
2 tablespoons light corn syrup
2½ cups finely crushed vanilla wafers

1. Preheat the oven to 350°F. Place pecans on a baking sheet, and toast for 5 to 7 minutes, or until lightly browned. Remove the pan from the oven, and finely chop nuts in a food processor using on-and-off pulsing, or by hand. Set aside.

2. Sift 1 cup sugar and cocoa powder into a mixing bowl, and whisk in bourbon and corn syrup. Stir in cookie crumbs and chopped nuts, and mix well. Refrigerate mixture for 30 minutes.

3. Sift remaining sugar into a low bowl. Make mixture into 1-inch balls, and roll balls in the sugar to coat evenly. Refrigerate balls for a minimum of 4 hours.

Note: The balls can be stored refrigerated up to 2 weeks. Place them in an airtight container with sheets of plastic wrap in between the layers.

Variations:
* Use rum instead of bourbon.
* Use Frangelico instead of bourbon; hazelnuts rather than pecans. These can be made with or without the cocoa.
* Use Grand Marnier instead of bourbon, omit the cocoa, and add 1 tablespoon grated orange zest.
* Add 1 cup finely chopped bittersweet chocolate or miniature chocolate chips.
* Roll balls in additional finely chopped nuts instead of confectioners' sugar.
* Use ginger snaps or crushed chocolate cookies instead of vanilla wafers.
* Omit the cocoa, use rum and add ¾ cup toasted coconut.
* Add ½ teaspoon ground cinnamon or apple pie spice.
* Add ¾ cup finely chopped raisins or other dried fruit.

> Legend has it that bourbon balls were first made before World War II in Kentucky, where, of course, bourbon was used. The "inventor" of mixing candy with bourbon was Ruth Hanly Booe, who, along with other former teacher Rebecca Gooch, began a candy company in Frankfort, Kentucky, in 1919.

Chocolate Kahlúa Balls

The combination of chocolate with coconut and laced with heady liqueur is a grown-up delight.

Makes 4 dozen | Active time: 30 minutes | Start to finish: 4½ hours, including 4 hours to chill

1 cup macadamia nuts

1½ cups shredded sweetened coconut

6 ounces good quality bittersweet chocolate

½ cup evaporated milk

Pinch of salt

2½ cups chocolate cookie crumbs

½ cup confectioners' sugar

½ cup Kahlúa liqueur

½ teaspoon pure vanilla extract

1. Preheat the oven to 350°F. Place macadamia nuts on a baking sheet, and toast for 5 to 7 minutes, or until lightly browned. Remove the pan from the oven, and finely chop nuts in a food processor using on-and-off pulsing, or by hand. Set aside. Place coconut on another baking pan, and toast for 10 to 12 minutes, or until browned. Remove the pan from the oven, and set aside.

2. Break chocolate into pieces no larger than a lima bean. Either chop chocolate in a food processor using on-and-off pulsing, or place it in a heavy resealable plastic bag, and smash it with the back of a heavy skillet.

3. Heat evaporated milk in a saucepan over medium heat, stirring frequently, until mixture comes to a simmer. Stir in salt, and add chocolate. Remove the pan from the heat, cover the pan, and allow chocolate to melt for 5 minutes.

4. Scrape chocolate mixture into a mixing bowl, and add nuts, cookie crumbs, confectioners' sugar, Kahlúa, and vanilla, and mix well. Refrigerate mixture for 30 minutes.

5. Place coconut in a low bowl. Make mixture into 1-inch balls, and roll balls in the sugar to coat evenly. Refrigerate balls for a minimum of 4 hours.

Note: The balls can be stored refrigerated up to 2 weeks. Place them in an airtight container with sheets of plastic wrap in between the layers.

Variations:

* Use crushed ginger snap cookies or crushed vanilla cookies instead of chocolate cookie crumbs.
* Use Grand Marnier and add ½ cup finely chopped dried apricots.
* Use almonds, pecans, or hazelnuts rather than the macadamia nuts.

The Aztecs first discovered chocolate, and our word comes from the Aztec *xocolatl*, which means "bitter water." Famed King Montezuma believed chocolate was an aphrodisiac and is reported to have consumed some 50 cups a day.

Crispy Peanut Butter Balls

The granola you choose to make these healthful snack balls changes the nature of the mixture.

Makes 2 dozen | Active time: 10 minutes | Start to finish: 40 minutes, including 30 minutes to chill

½ cup peanut butter

3 tablespoons honey

2 cups granola cereal or muesli

2 to 4 tablespoons freshly squeezed orange juice

1 tablespoon grated orange zest

Vegetable oil spray

1. Whisk peanut butter and honey in mixing bowl until smooth. Add granola, orange juice, and orange zest, and stir with a strong spatula until mixed well. Add additional orange juice, if necessary, so mixture stays together.

2. Spray your hands with vegetable oil spray. Make mixture into 1½-inch balls, and arrange balls on a baking sheet. Refrigerate for a minimum of 30 minutes.

Note: The balls can be stored refrigerated up to 1 week. Place them in an airtight container with sheets of plastic wrap in between the layers.

Variations:

* Top with a dollop of brandy sauce.
* Use milk instead of orange juice, omit the orange zest, and add ½ teaspoon ground cinnamon to the peanut butter and honey mixture before adding the cereal.
* Substitute almond butter for the peanut butter. If using natural almond butter, add ½ cup confectioners' sugar.
* Add ¾ cup chopped dried fruit.
* Add ¾ cup miniature chocolate chips or butterscotch chips.

Peanuts, which are actually a legume and not a nut, are used in cuisines around the world, but peanut butter is an American invention, developed in 1890 and first promoted as a health food at the 1904 World's Fair in St. Louis.

Dried Fruit Coconut Balls

Not all calories are created equal, and the fat calories in these treats are monounsaturated from the nuts, so they can be eaten without much guilt. The combination of fruits along with the sweet honey is really satisfying.

Makes 2½ dozen | Active time: 25 minutes | Start to finish: 55 minutes, including 30 minutes to chill

1 cup cashews pieces
1½ cups shredded sweetened coconut
½ cup finely chopped dried apricots
½ cup dried currants
½ cup finely chopped dried dates
½ cup graham cracker crumbs
⅓ cup honey
Vegetable oil spray

1. Preheat the oven to 350°F. Place cashews on a baking sheet, and toast for 5 to 7 minutes, or until lightly browned. Remove the pan from the oven, and finely chop nuts in a food processor using on-and-off pulsing, or by hand. Set aside. Place coconut on another baking pan, and toast for 10 to 12 minutes, or until browned. Remove the pan from the oven, and set aside.

2. Combine cashews, ½ cup coconut, dried apricots, dried currants, chopped dates, graham cracker crumbs, and honey in a mixing bowl. Stir with a strong spatula until mixed well. Add additional honey, if necessary, so mixture stays together.

3. Spray your hands with vegetable oil spray, and place remaining coconut in a shallow bowl. Make mixture into 2-inch balls, roll balls in coconut, and arrange balls on a baking sheet. Refrigerate for a minimum of 30 minutes.

Note: The balls can be stored refrigerated up to 1 week. Place them in an airtight container with sheets of plastic wrap in between the layers.

Variations:
✳ Use any combination of dried fruits.
✳ Add some shredded sweetened coconut.
✳ Substitute any variety of nut.
✳ Substitute crushed ginger snaps for the graham cracker crumbs.

When measuring sticky ingredients like honey or molasses, spray the measuring cup with a non-flavored vegetable oil spray. The sticky stuff will pour right out.

Mexican Wedding Cookies

Sometimes called *polvarones*, these rich and buttery cookies similar to shortbread. In Mexico they are made with lard, but I prefer unsalted butter.

Makes 3 dozen | *Active time: 20 minutes* | *Start to finish: 45 minutes*

½ pound (2 sticks) unsalted butter, softened

1¾ cups confectioners' sugar, divided

1 cup cake flour

1 cup self-rising flour

1 cup blanched almonds, very finely chopped

½ teaspoon pure vanilla extract

1. Preheat the oven to 350°F. Grease 2 baking sheets with butter.

2. Place butter in a mixing bowl with 1¼ cups sugar, and beat well at medium speed with an electric mixer until light and fluffy. Add cake flour, self-rising flour, almonds, and vanilla to the bowl, and mix briefly until just combined. The dough will be very stiff; add a few drops of hot water, if necessary, to make it pliable.

3. Form dough into ¾-inch balls, and place them 1 inch apart on the prepared baking sheets. Bake for 15 to 18 minutes, or until firm. Remove the pans from the oven.

4. Sift remaining sugar into a low bowl, and add a few cookies at a time, rolling them around in the sugar to coat them well. Transfer cookies to a rack to cool completely.

Note: The cookies can be stored in an airtight container at room temperature up to 3 days, or they can be frozen up to 3 months.

Variation:

＊ Use pecans or walnuts in place of the almonds. Toast them in a 350°F oven for 5 to 7 minutes before chopping them.

> If your butter is too cold to work into dough, don't soften it in the microwave oven. A few seconds too long and you've got a melted mess. Grate cold butter on the large holes of a box grater. It will soften in a matter of minutes.

Eggnog Fritters with Maple Sauce

Eggnog, flavored with spices and brandy, is not only a holiday treat, it lends flavor to these crispy fritters any time of year.

Makes 2 dozen | *Active time: 20 minutes* | *Start to finish: 20 minutes*

2 large eggs

1 cup whole milk

¼ cup brandy, divided

1¼ teaspoons pure vanilla extract, divided

2½ cups all-purpose flour

½ cup granulated sugar

2 teaspoons baking powder

1 teaspoon baking soda

1 teaspoon apple pie spice

Pinch of salt

1 cup pure maple syrup

2 tablespoons brandy

½ teaspoon ground cinnamon

3 cups vegetable oil for frying

1. Whisk eggs, milk, 2 tablespoons brandy, and ¾ teaspoon vanilla in a mixing bowl. Combine flour, sugar, baking powder, baking soda, apple pie spice, and salt in another mixing bowl, and whisk well. Stir dry ingredients into wet ingredients, stirring until just combined.

2. Combine maple syrup, remaining 2 tablespoons brandy, remaining ½ teaspoon vanilla, and cinnamon in a small saucepan, and whisk well. Heat to a simmer, and set aside.

3. Heat oil in a deep-sided saucepan or deep-fryer to a temperature of 375ºF. Preheat the oven to 150°F, and line a baking sheet with paper towels.

4. Using a rubber spatula, push batter off carefully into hot fat, about 1 tablespoonful at a time. Fry fritters until they are a deep golden brown, turning them in the hot fat to brown both sides. Remove fritters from the pan with a slotted spoon, and drain on paper towel-lined baking sheet. Keep fritters warm in the oven while frying remaining batter. Serve immediately, passing maple sauce separately.

Note: The fritters can be prepared up to 2 days in advance and refrigerated, tightly covered. Reheat in a 375°F oven for 5 to 7 minutes, or until hot and crispy.

Variations:
* Use Grand Marnier and 2 teaspoons orange zest in place of the brandy and apples.
* Want a lighter flavor than maple? Try a fruit puree sauce sweetened with the same flavor as a jam.

Early New England settlers sweetened foods with maple syrup because expensive white sugar had to be imported. Tapping the sugar maple trees native to North America and cooking syrup from the sap is another skill the Native Americans taught the settlers.

Italian Sweet Ricotta Fritters

These fritters are light and delicious, with just a hint of orange.

Makes 2 dozen | *Active time: 20 minutes* | *Start to finish: 20 minutes*

4 large eggs

⅓ cup granulated sugar

1 pound ricotta cheese

2 teaspoons grated orange zest

½ teaspoon pure vanilla extract

1 tablespoon baking powder

Pinch of salt

1 cup all-purpose flour

3 cups vegetable oil for frying

½ cup confectioners' sugar

1. Combine eggs, sugar, ricotta, orange zest, and vanilla in the bowl of an electric mixer, and beat at medium speed until smooth. Add baking powder and salt, and mix well. Add flour and mix at low speed until just combined.

2. Heat oil in a deep-sided saucepan or deep-fryer to a temperature of 375°F. Preheat the oven to 150°F, and line a baking sheet with paper towels.

3. Using a rubber spatula, push batter off carefully into hot fat, about 1 tablespoonful at a time. Fry fritters until they are a deep golden brown, turning them in the hot fat to brown both sides. Remove fritters from the pan with a slotted spoon, and drain on paper towel-lined baking sheet. Keep fritters warm in the oven while frying remaining batter. Serve immediately dusted with confectioners' sugar.

Note: The fritters can be prepared up to 2 days in advance and refrigerated, tightly covered. Reheat in a 375°F oven for 5 to 7 minutes, or until hot and crispy.

Variations:

* Omit the orange zest and add ½ teaspoon ground cinnamon and a pinch of ground nutmeg.
* Add ½ cup finely chopped dried fruit to the fritter batter.
* Rather than dusting the fritters with confectioners' sugar, drizzle heated honey over the top.

> If you live in a neighborhood with an Italian grocery store, see if it carries fresh ricotta cheese; it has a creamy flavor and texture not found in commercial cheeses.

Banana Fritters

I love dessert fritters with their crispy coating! Serve them plain—or with ice cream.

Makes 2 dozen | *Active time: 20 minutes* | *Start to finish: 20 minutes*

1 large egg

½ cup whole milk

1½ cups chopped ripe bananas

1⅓ cups all-purpose flour

3 tablespoons granulated sugar

1½ teaspoons baking powder

½ teaspoon ground cinnamon

½ teaspoon ground ginger

Pinch of salt

3 cups vegetable oil for frying

Confectioners' sugar for dusting the fritters

1. Whisk egg and milk in a mixing bowl, and stir in bananas. Combine flour, sugar, baking powder, cinnamon, ginger, and salt in another mixing bowl, and whisk well. Stir dry ingredients into banana mixture, stirring until just combined.

2. Heat oil in a deep-sided saucepan or deep-fryer to a temperature of 375°F. Preheat the oven to 150°F. Line a baking sheet with paper towels.

3. Using a rubber spatula push batter off carefully into hot fat, about 1 tablespoonful at a time. Fry fritters until they are a deep golden brown, turning them in the hot fat to brown both sides. Remove fritters from the pan with a slotted spoon, and drain on paper towel-lined baking sheet.Keep fritters warm in the oven while frying remaining batter. Serve immediately dusted with confectioners' sugar.

Note: The fritters can be prepared up to 2 days in advance and refrigerated, tightly covered. Reheat in a 375°F oven for 5 to 7 minutes, or until hot and crispy.

Variations:

∗ Use any juicy fruit; I've used a combination of banana and mango or pineapple and peaches with fresh raspberries.

∗ Replace 2 tablespoons of milk with rum or a liqueur.

Index

About Cider Mill Press
Book Publishers

Good ideas ripen with time. From seed to harvest, Cider Mill Press brings fine reading, information, and entertainment together between the covers of its creatively crafted books. Our Cider Mill bears fruit twice a year, publishing a new crop of titles each spring and fall.

"Where Good Books Are Ready for Press"

Visit us on the Web at
www.cidermillpress.com
or write to us at
12 Spring Street
PO Box 454
Kennebunkport, Maine 04046